PLANTS FOR HOUSTON
AND THE GULF COAST

PLANTS FOR HOUSTON
AND THE
GULF COAST

HOWARD GARRETT

University of Texas Press

Austin

Printed in China
First edition, 2008

Requests for permission to reproduce material from this work should be sent to:
Permissions
University of Texas Press
P.O. Box 7819
Austin, TX 78713-7819
www.utexas.edu/utpress/about/bpermission.html

♾ The paper used in this book meets the minimum requirements of ANSI/NISO Z39.48-1992 (R1997) (Permanence of Paper).

Library of Congress Cataloging-in-Publication Data
Garrett, Howard, 1947–
Plants for Houston and the Gulf Coast / Howard Garrett. — 1st ed.
p. cm.
Includes bibliographical references and index.
ISBN 978-0-292-71740-4 (pbk. : alk. paper)
1. Landscape plants—Texas—Houston. 2. Landscape plants—Gulf Coast Region (U.S.) 3. Landscape gardening—Texas—Houston. 4. Landscape gardening—Gulf Coast Region (U.S.) 5. Organic gardening—Texas—Houston. 6. Organic gardening—Gulf Coast Region (U.S.) I. Title.

SB435.52.T4.G36 2008
635.909764'1411—dc22

2007037412

*To the women of the River Oaks Garden Club and
the Garden Club of Houston*

CONTENTS

Introduction   1

Planting Design   2

Plant Installation—The Natural Way   5

Plant Maintenance   18

    Maintenance by the Calendar   28

Trees   40

Shrubs and "Sort of" Shrubs   75

Ground Covers and Vines   101

Annuals and Perennials   114

Grasses   142

Recommended Reading   147

Index   149

Several plant people in Houston have been a great help with this book.
Some of those friends include Hedi Sheesley of Treesearch Farms, John Ferguson
of Nature's Way, Carter and J. C. Taylor of Condon Gardens, Jason McKenzie
of Pineywoods Nursery, and Beverly Welch of the Arbor Gate.

PLANTS FOR HOUSTON
AND THE GULF COAST

INTRODUCTION

A GARDENING BOOK IS ONLY USEFUL if it has accurate information and helpful photos. Being able to see what the plants look like was one of the secrets of my first book, *Plants of the Metroplex*. I wrote it in 1974, and it is still selling well today.

Sorry it has taken me so long to do a similar book for Houston and the Gulf Coast, but here it is. If you have any complaints or comments, please send them to me at info@dirtdoctor.com. I continue to update and improve all my books.

I'm an organic guy, and I have been delighted to discover that the natural alternatives really work. Organic gardening is not a fad. Many in the universities and some on the radio will tell you that total organic programs won't work. They are wrong. There is no reason at all to use toxic synthetic pesticides or salt-based synthetic fertilizers. Everything about the natural organic program works better. Plants have less stress, and fewer transplant losses occur. Plants have fewer insect pests and disease problems. Plants also have significantly more tolerance to weather stress—both heat and cold. Organic gardeners have more fun and save money.

We are poisoning the environment with artificial fertilizers and in the process growing sick plants. These fertilizers are causing a toxic buildup of nitrates and other harmful salts in the soil and drinking water. Farmers and home gardeners need to change. Artificial fertilizers harm or destroy the beneficial microorganisms in the soil, force-feed plants, and cause plants to attract insects. It shouldn't be a surprise to anyone that Mother Nature knows best.

Although I didn't realize it in the beginning, my plant material recommendations have always included a high percentage of native plants—I just didn't identify them as such. I also strongly believe that certain introduced plants are excellent and some even superior to their native counterparts. Using a careful mixture of both native and adapted introductions is sensible for most gardens. On the other hand, using natives when possible is advisable.

Three kinds of plants are covered here: (1) recommended plants, (2) plants that can be used but aren't highly recommended, and (3) plants that are not recommended and should not be planted. I am not noncommittal about plants. My likes, dislikes, and experiences with all the plants are always expressed. The simple identification of the various plants isn't really worth much. The value I hope you receive from this book results from the editorial pros and cons based on my experience with the almost *400 plants* discussed. The detailed information on each plant should help you design, plant, and maintain your garden. The plants with photos at the text are the top recommendations. Although no plant or technique is perfect, my recommendations should give you beautiful results and great enjoyment from a new or renovated garden.

PLANTING DESIGN

GARDENS

SHOULD BE

ALLOWED TO

CHANGE

OVER TIME—

THEY'RE GOING

TO ANYWAY!

A GARDEN HAS AT LEAST TWO LIVES—the first when it is installed, the second when the trees mature and shade the ground. When the trees are young, the majority of the shrubs, ground covers, and grasses must be those that thrive in the full sun. Later, as the trees grow and mature, the situation changes. Shade becomes the order of the day, and the low plants and understory trees must be shade tolerant. By far one of my most common questions is how to grow grass in shady conditions. Both the grass and the trees want the sunlight. Guess which one will win out. At this point, shade-tolerant ground covers and shrubs need to be used, or trees must be heavily pruned or removed. I don't recommend the second approach much.

Landscape gardens are never static. They are dynamic and continue to change with age. One of the great pleasures of gardening is fine-tuning the landscaping by moving plants about, adding plants when needed and removing those that are no longer useful.

Creating successful landscaping is not difficult if certain basic steps are taken: (1) careful selection of native and well-adapted plant types; (2) organic bed preparation; (3) drainage solutions; (4) organic planting techniques; (5) organic maintenance procedures.

TREES

Trees are the first consideration in landscape design. A tree is the only home improvement that can return many times the cost of the original investment. In addition to adding beauty, trees create the atmosphere or feel of a garden. They invite us, shade us, surprise us, house wildlife, create backgrounds and niches, inspire and humble us. Besides increasing in value as they grow, trees save energy and money by shading our houses in the summer and by letting the sun shine through for warmth in the winter.

There are two categories of trees: shade and ornamental. Shade trees are the large structural trees that form the skeleton of the planting plan and grow to be 40' to 100' tall. They are used to create the outdoor spaces, block undesirable views, and provide shade. This category includes the oaks, elms, pecans, and other long-lived trees. Of all the plants, shade trees provide the greatest long-term value, so their use should be carefully considered and given a large percentage of the landscape budget.

Ornamental trees are those used for aesthetics, to create focal points, and they grow to be 8' to 30' tall. Trees such as crabapple, hawthorn, and crape myrtle are used primarily for their spring or summer flower color. Others, such as yaupon or wax myrtle, are used for their evergreen color or berries. Some, such as Japanese maple, are used for their distinctive foliage color and interesting branching characteristics.

SHRUBS

Shrubs should be selected on the basis of what variety will grow best in the space provided. If more than one variety will work, this decision becomes subjective based on the desire for flowers, interesting foliage, fall color, etc. However, horticultural requirements should be the prerequisite and have priority over aesthetic considerations. Tall-growing varieties are used for background plantings and screens. Medium-height shrubs are used for flower display or evergreen color. Dwarf varieties are used for masses and interesting bed shapes.

GROUND COVERS

Ground-cover plants are low-growing, vinelike, and grasslike materials that are primarily used to cover large areas of ground. They are best used where grass won't grow and for creating interesting bed shapes. Ground covers are usually the best choice in heavily shaded areas. Often the ground covers become the last phase of the permanent garden installation and are planted after the trees have matured to shade the ground.

VINES

Vines are usually fast-growing plants that twine or cling to climb vertically on walls, fences, posts, or overhead structures. They are used for quick shade, vertical softening, or colorful flower display. Vines are an inexpensive way to have lots of greenery and color in a hurry. They are also quite good in smaller spaces where wide-growing shrubs and trees would be a problem.

HERBS

Herbs make wonderful landscape plants and should be used more in ornamental gardens even if gourmet cooking is not in the plans. The traditional definition of "herb" is any plant that is used to flavor foods, provide medicinal properties, offer up fragrances or that has any other use besides looking pretty. Herbs fall into several categories—shrubs, ground covers, annuals, and perennials—and are therefore distributed throughout the pages of this book.

FLOWERS

Flowers are an important finishing touch to any fine garden. Everyone loves colorful flowers. Annuals are useful for that dramatic splash of one-season color, and the perennials are valuable because of their faithful return to bloom year after year. Since replacing annual color each year is expensive, annuals should be concentrated in one or a few spots rather than scattering them all about. The perennial flowers can be used more randomly throughout the garden.

TREES, IF USED PROPERLY AND NOT SIMPLY SCATTERED OUT ALL OVER THE SITE, FUNCTION AS THE WALLS AND ROOFS OF OUR OUTDOOR ROOMS.

SUN GARDENS ARE EASILY THE MOST COLORFUL.

SHADE GARDENS ARE THE EASIEST TO MAINTAIN— LESS WATERING AND FEWER WEEDS TO FIGHT.

NATIVE AND INTRODUCED PLANTS CAN AND SHOULD BE USED TOGETHER. BIODIVERSITY IS AN IMPORTANT ASPECT OF PROPER DESIGN AND PROPER HORTICULTURE.

GRASSES

Grasses should be selected on horticultural requirements. Large sunny areas that will have active use should use common Bermudagrass or buffalograss. Shady, less-used areas should use St. Augustine and centipede grass. Areas that will not have much water should use buffalograss. Areas that need a smooth, highly refined surface should use the hybrid tifgrasses or paspalum.

SPECIAL NOTE

Many poisonous plants exist. Children need to be taught which plants can be eaten and which are dangerous. It is best to not let them eat any plants without your approval and supervision.

PLANT INSTALLATION— THE NATURAL WAY

SOILS

First, some basic information on soils. Properties in Houston have one or a combination of soil types: clay, silt, loam, sandy loam, sand, gravel, and rock. Clay soils have the smallest particles, compact the most, and drain the least. Sand, gravel, and broken rock have the largest particles, compact the least, and drain the best. Soil contains five major components: organic material, minerals, water, air, and living organisms. The living organisms are very important and consist of worms, insects, plants, algae, bacteria, fungi, and other microorganisms. Loose, organic, well-drained, biologically active soils are best.

Tightly structured clays of the Gulf Coast are nutritious soils, but they need to be loosened to improve drainage and allow oxygen into the root zone. These soils also need large quantities of organic matter, which leads to increased life in the soil, which leads to fertilizer elements and trace minerals being available to plant roots.

Healthy soils must also have a balance of minerals. A soil test will show the percentage of the mineral nutrients. A balanced soil should have approximately the following percentages of available nutrients: 68% calcium, 12% magnesium, 5% potassium, and adequate amounts of all the other mineral elements, including sulfur, iron, copper, zinc, molybdenum, boron, and manganese. If the mineral balance of the soil is correct, the pH at the surface of the soil will be between 6.3 and 6.8. A pH of 7.0 is neutral. Starting with a soil test can be helpful, but if quality compost and other organic amendments are used, Nature will balance the soil for you.

THE FIRST SIX INCHES OF SOILS IS WHERE MOST ROOTS RESIDE AND IS A LIVING AND CONSTANTLY CHANGING ENVIRONMENT.

SOIL AMENDMENTS

Recommended soil amendments are those materials that improve the chemistry, physics, and biological activity of the soil. All soils can be improved by increasing the living organisms. The life makes it all happen. Clay soils are basically deficient in two things—air and organic matter. Sandy soils are deficient in everything but sand. Both soils need the same additions for building the life in the soil. The amendments I recommend, in order of importance, are as follows:

- **Organic material** helps balance the chemical and physical nature of the soil. The best organic matter for bed preparation is compost. Compost can be made from anything that was once alive. Organic matter provides humus and aids in the loosening of the soil by adding larger particles than the soil particles and by providing food for microorganisms. Life in the soil is the key to nutrients and trace minerals being available to plants. Compost tea is an efficient way to build organic matter.

EIGHTY-FIVE
PERCENT OF A
PLANT'S ROOTS ARE
FOUND IN THE
FIRST SIX INCHES
OF SOIL. THERE-
FORE THERE'S NO
NEED TO WORK
ORGANIC MATERIAL
INTO THE SOIL
VERY DEEPLY.

■ **Greensand** is a marine deposit called glauconite, which is iron potassium sili-cate and an excellent source of trace minerals. Most greensand contains 15%–20% iron as well as many other available trace minerals. It is excellent for plants that are yellow due to trace mineral deficiencies.

■ **Lava sand** is the smaller waste material left from lava gravel manufacturing. It is an excellent, highly paramagnetic soil amendment material. It can be used in potting soils and bed preparation for all landscaping and food crops. Finer-textured material would be even better if it were easily available. This is one of the most controversial products I recommend. All the hardheaded organi-phobes have to do to see its power is—try it!

■ **Cornmeal** has a terrific use in gardening, landscaping, and farming—even for your potted plants. It is a natural disease control. Dr. Joe McFarland and his staff at the A&M Research Station in Stephenville discovered that cornmeal is effective at controlling fungal diseases on peanuts. I started playing with it and discovered that it is effective on brown patch in St. Augustine and on damp-ing-off in seedlings. Used at about 20 lbs. per 1,000 sq. ft. of surface area of soil, horticultural or whole ground cornmeal will help control all diseases on photinia, Indian hawthorn, roses, fruit trees, turf, and seed flats. Whole ground cornmeal contains the entire corn kernel. Unfortunately, the grocery store cornmeal is only the starchy inside of the corn kernel and not nearly as effective.

Soil Amendments

Close examination shows the difference in soil particle sizes. Clay particles are smallest. Silt particles are inter-mediate, and sand particles are coars-est. Loam soil con-tains a blend of all three sizes.

- **Dry molasses** isn't really straight dried molasses. It is molasses sprayed on an organic residue carrier like small bits of soy. It's an excellent carbon and carbohydrate source that stimulates beneficial microorganisms, and it repels fire ants.

- **Expanded shale** is made from natural shale ground into 1" or smaller particles and then kiln fired. As it progresses through the kiln for 40 minutes at 2,000 degrees C, certain chemical processes take place in the silica content (60%–70%), causing the material to expand. As the material cools, cavities are left after gases escape, leaving a porous lightweight chunk capable of absorbing water and releasing it slowly at a later time. It is an excellent amendment for loosening tight soils and stimulating growth.

- **Liquid molasses** is a liquid carbohydrate used as a soil amendment to feed and stimulate microorganisms. It contains sulfur, potash, and many trace minerals. Molasses provides food for microorganisms and is a source of carbon, sulfur, and potash. It is a good, quick source of energy for the soil life and microbes in a compost pile, and will chase fire ants away. It is a carbon source and feeds beneficial microbes, creating greater natural fertility. Liquid molasses is used in sprays and drenches. It is an excellent foliar-feeding material and can be mixed with other organic liquids. Use at 1–2 gallons per acre for soil application. For foliar application on broadleaf plants, use at 1–2 ounces per gallon of water. For grasses and grains, use 2–4 quarts per acre. Blackstrap molasses, which is hard to find, is the best choice because it contains the sulfur and iron of the original material, but any molasses will work.

  My least favorite organic matter for bed preparation is peat moss because it is antimicrobial, is the most expensive organic material, and must be purchased from sources that are several hundred miles outside Texas. An environmental consideration also exists related to the harvesting of peat moss from bogs.

- **Fertilizers** are available in two forms: organic and synthetic. Organic fertilizers are the products of decayed plants and animals. They contain smaller amounts of N-P-K (nitrogen, phosphorus, and potassium) than do synthetic fertilizers, but they can contain all the trace minerals that are needed by plants—that's because they come from living organisms. Organic fertilizers all have natural slow release and provide humus for the soil. Synthetic fertilizers are man-made harsh chemical products and are water-soluble, salt-based, too high in nitrogen, and lacking in trace minerals. They are completely unbalanced because they contain no carbon energy. They should not be used.

MULCHES

Organic materials also have another important function—as mulch. Mulches are used to cover the bare soil after planting has been done. My favorite is coarsely shredded tree trimmings. Other available mulches include straw, pine needles, decomposed sawdust, cotton seed hulls, pecan hulls, and wood chips.

I don't like pine bark, cypress, plastics, fabrics, or gravel in most cases. Lava

A PLANT'S HEALTH DEPENDS ON THE SOIL'S ABILITY TO DRAIN AWAY EXCESS WATER. IF WATER FILLS THE PORES IN THE SOIL, THERE IS NO ROOM FOR OXYGEN.

gravel is the only good choice in this category. They are much harder on the plants and are unattractive. They also don't break down into humus for the soil. Pine bark is my least favorite organic mulch because its flat pieces are easily washed or blown away. Pine bark also produces some pretty nasty natural chemicals as it breaks down. The best mulches are shredded tree trimmings from your own property; the second best are purchased and come from other properties. Partially composted shredded tree trimmings mixed with finished compost is the best mulch of all.

USING THE ORGANIC TOOLS

BUILD THE ORGANIC MATTER

Increase the health of the soil by using quality compost, earthworm castings, and organic fertilizers to increase the organic matter. Mulch all plantings. Maintain an organic mulch layer on the bare soil year-round. Avoid all synthetic fertilizers that contain no organic matter. These fake fertilizers not only don't build the soil health, they injure the soil and plant roots with every application.

BUILD THE MINERAL CONTENT

Balance the minerals in the soil by applying rock powders or sands that provide the major nutrients and trace minerals needed by plants to be healthy. Volcanic rock materials are especially important because they provide much more than minerals. The best choices include lava sand, Texas greensand, soft rock phosphate, granite sand, zeolite, basalt, natural diatomaceous earth, and other natural mineral sources.

ENCOURAGE BIODIVERSITY

Healthy gardens, farms, and ranches need a mix of plants and animals. Monocultures of plants are often very productive for a while but later succumb to insects and diseases. Examples include the Irish potato blight, Dutch elm disease, and more recently oak wilt here in Texas. Monocultures lack the genetic diversity to respond to changing environmental threats and thus become sitting ducks for parasites, predators, and pathogens. Stop using all products that do damage to the life in the soil. Encourage life.

ADD MOLASSES

Sugar, especially in the form of molasses, is an effective soil amendment. These carbohydrates provide food for the beneficial microorganisms. Using sugar heavily should not be done on a continuing basis, but it is highly effective in the early stages of the program. Small amounts of molasses are effective in the long term and are often found in quality organic liquid and dry fertilizers.

PLANTING

In general, the ideal time to plant trees, shrubs, and spring-blooming perennials is fall; second best is anytime in the winter; third is the spring; last is in the heat of

THE KEY TO PLANT HEALTH IS THE HEALTH OF THE SOIL. ORGANIC FERTILIZERS ARE NOT USED TO FORCE-FEED PLANTS. THEY ARE USED TO STIMULATE BIOLOGICAL ACTIVITY, WHICH CREATES THE NATURAL FERTILITY.

summer. Planting in the fall or winter offers roots a chance to start growing before the foliage emerges in the spring. Fall is the ideal tree and shrub planting time.

USE ADAPTED PLANTS

Planting well-adapted plants is the most important step. Unless you select adapted plants, it doesn't matter whether your program is organic or toxic. The best choices are the natives, but the well-adapted introductions and naturalized plants are also good.

PLANTING TIMES

Most plants can be planted any month of the year if the following precautions are taken:

- **Hot part of summer:** When transporting plants in an open vehicle, cover to protect the foliage from the sun and wind and keep the root ball moist. Always dampen the planting beds prior to planting.

- **Freezing weather:** Don't leave plants out of the ground during extreme cold without protecting the roots from possible freeze damage. Store plants in sunny areas prior to planting. Always keep the plants moist and mulched during freezing weather. Once in the ground, plants will normally survive a freeze.

- **Mild weather:** The mild weather can make you forget to keep containers or newly planted material moist, so check often but do not overwater.

TREE PLANTING

Trees are by far the most important landscape element. They create the garden space and are the skeleton or framework for everything else that happens. They are also the only landscape element that appreciates greatly in value through the years.

There's only one catch. If the trees aren't healthy and don't grow, they won't do you any good at all. To grow properly, trees must be planted properly. Many tree-planting procedures not only are horticulturally incorrect but are substantial wastes of money. My recommendations for tree planting have developed over years of carefully studying many planting techniques and trying to understand what works and what doesn't.

The first time I saw trees planted correctly was in 1976. I had been commissioned to design the landscaping for the Harris Corporation on Dallas North Parkway in Addison, Texas. The budget was tight and the site was large and uninteresting. Utilizing the excess soil from the building excavation, free-flowing berms were created to add interest and provide sites for trees to be planted. I didn't realize at the time the importance of the built-in drainage system the berms provided.

An old friend, Cody Carter, planted all the trees on that job. Since that time, I've watched those trees and I've watched trees on other projects planted using all kinds of various techniques. Here's what I learned and recommend.

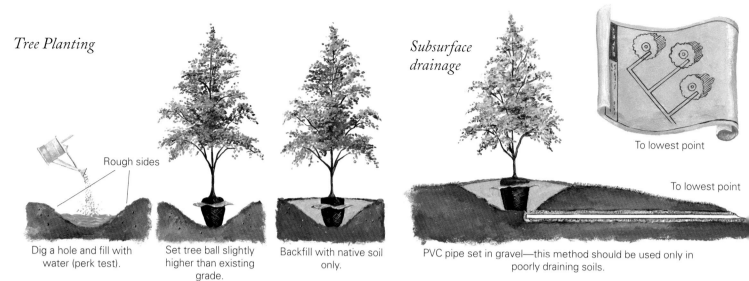

Tree Planting

Rough sides

Dig a hole and fill with water (perk test).

Set tree ball slightly higher than existing grade.

Backfill with native soil only.

Subsurface drainage

To lowest point

To lowest point

PVC pipe set in gravel—this method should be used only in poorly draining soils.

Gravel Sump

Gravel

Rock

1. DIG AN UGLY HOLE

The hole should be dug exactly the same depth as the height of the ball. Don't guess—actually measure the height of the ball. Never plant trees in slick-sided or glazed holes such as those caused by a tree spade or auger, unless the slick sides are destroyed at planting. Holes with glazed sides greatly restrict root penetration into the surrounding soil, can cause circling roots, and consequently limit proper root development.

2. RUN A PERK TEST

Simply fill the hole with water and wait until the next day. If the water level doesn't drain away overnight, a drainage problem is indicated. At this point, the tree needs to be moved to another location or have drainage added in the form of a PVC drain line set in gravel running from the hole to a lower point on the site. Another draining method that sometimes works is a pier hole dug down from the bottom of the hole into a different soil type and filled with gravel. A sump from the top of the ball down to the bottom of the ball does little if any good. Positive drainage is critical, so don't shortcut this step. Spraying the sides of the holes with Garrett Juice or hydrogen peroxide will help initial root establishment.

3. PLANT HIGH

Most trees are planted too deep in the ground. The root flare is part of the trunk and should be placed above ground. Remove burlap, excess soil, and mulch from the surface to expose the true top of the ball. Place the tree in the center of the hole, making sure that the top of the ball is slightly higher than the surrounding grade. Remove the excess soil from the top of the root ball and any "bird's nest" or circling roots.

4. BACKFILL WITH EXISTING SOIL

Backfill with the soil that was removed from the hole. This is a critical point. Do not add sand, foreign soil, organic matter, or fertilizer into the backfill. The roots need to start growing in the native soil from the beginning. When the hole is dug in solid rock, topsoil from the same area should be used. Some native rock mixed into the backfill is beneficial. Adding amendments such as peat moss, sand, or foreign soils to the backfill not only wastes money but is detrimental to the tree. Putting gravel in the bottom of the hole is a total waste of money.

When planting balled and burlapped plants, remove the burlap from the top of the ball. Remove any nylon or plastic covering or string, since these materials do not decompose and can girdle the trunk and roots as the plant grows. Studies have shown that even wire mesh should be removed to avoid root girdling because wire does not break down very fast in our alkaline soils, especially below 10 inches.

When planting from plastic containers, carefully remove plants and tear the outside roots if they have grown solidly against the container. Never leave plants in containers. Bare-rooted, balled and burlapped, and container plant materials should be planted the same way. Removing all the soil from container-grown plants is now something I recommend. When planting bare-rooted plants, it is critical to keep the roots moist during the transportation and planting process.

Planting Depths

After backfilling:
- Add 1" compost and organic sand.
- Add 3"–5" native cedar mulch.
- Do not pile mulch on trunks
- Do not stake trees.
- Do not wrap tree trunks
- Do not thin or top trees
- Do not build watering rings
- And *for sure*—don't build mulch "volcanoes" around tree trunks.

Note: Remove any soil that has been added to the top of root balls. Expose the actual top of the root ball.

Do not thin out or top tree.

Top of ball should be at least 2" higher than ground grade.

Shredded native cedar mulch

Width of ball (minimum)

Wide rough-sided hole

1" layer of compost and volcanic sand

Backfill with existing native soil, no amendments. Settle the soil with water, no tamping.

Tree ball to rest on existing native soil

DO NOT USE PLASTIC SHEETS OR FABRICS OF ANY KIND AROUND PLANTS AS MULCH OR FOR ANY OTHER REASON. THE PLANT'S ROOT SYSTEM WILL COOK FROM THE HEAT BUILDUP. PLASTIC ALSO CUTS OFF THE OXYGEN NEEDED BY THE SOIL. I ALSO DO NOT RECOMMEND RUBBER OR DYED WOOD AS MULCHES. NOTHING COMPARES TO A THICK LAYER OF SHREDDED NATIVE TREE TRIMMINGS.

5. SETTLE SOIL WITH WATER

Water the backfill very carefully, making sure to get rid of all air pockets. Do not tamp the soil, as air pockets will be formed and roots will be killed in those spots.

6. DO NOT WRAP OR STAKE

Trunks of newly planted trees should not be wrapped. It's a waste of money, looks unattractive, harbors insects, and leaves the bark weak when removed. Tree wrapping is similar to a bandage left on your finger too long. If you are worried about the unlikely possibility of sunburn, it's much better to paint the trunk with a diluted latex paint that matches the color of the bark. White is okay, too.

Staking and guying is usually unnecessary if the tree has been planted properly with the proper earth ball size of at least 9" of ball for each 1" of trunk diameter. Staking is a waste of money and detrimental to the proper trunk development of the plant. In rare circumstances (sandy soil, tall evergreen trees, etc.) where the tree needs to be staked for a while, connect the guy wires as low on the trunk as possible and remove the stakes as soon as possible. Never leave them on more than one growing season. Temporary staking should be done with strong wire and metal eyebolts screwed into the trunk. Staking should only be done as a last resort—it is unsightly and expensive, adds to mowing and trimming costs, and restricts the tree's ability to develop tensile strength in the trunk and trunk diameter. It can also cause damage to the cambium layer. Remove all tags from plants.

7. DO NOT PRUNE

It's very bad advice to prune at planting to compensate for the loss of roots during transplanting or planting. Most trees fare much better if all the limbs and foliage are left intact. The more foliage, the more food can be produced to build the root system. Even low limbs and foliage should be left on the tree for at least two growing seasons to aid root development. The health of the root system is the key to the overall health of the tree.

The only trees that seem to respond positively to thinning at the time of transplanting are field-collected live oak, yaupon holly, and a few other evergreens. Plants purchased in containers definitely need no pruning, and deciduous trees never need to be thinned.

8. MULCH THE TOP OF BALL

After planting, mulch the top of the ball with 1" of compost and then 3" of mulch tapering to 0" at the tree trunk. This step is important in lawn areas or in beds. Don't ever plant grass over the tree ball until the tree is established.

SHRUB, GROUND COVER, AND VINE PLANTING

Soil preparation is necessary for all shrubs, ground covers, and vines. Most of the soils in Houston have one or more of these three basic problems: (1) lack of humus and related biological activity; (2) density of the soil particles, causing drainage problems and lack of oxygen in the root zone; (3) sandy conditions that don't hold humus and mineral nutrients. To help overcome these problems, the following soil preparations are recommended:

BED PREPARATION

The shorthand version is as follows:

1) Scrape off and remove existing grass, weeds, and other unneeded plants. Removed materials should be put in the compost pile.
2) Add 4"–6" of high-quality biologically active compost.
3) Add organic fertilizer at 20 lbs. per 1,000 sq. ft.
4) Add whole ground cornmeal and dry molasses at 20 lbs. per 1,000 sq. ft. each.
5) Add one or more of the following rock/mineral products: lava sand, basalt, decomposed granite, greensand, and expanded shale.
6) Till the new materials into existing soil to a depth of 8"–10".
7) Mulch all plantings about 1½"–2" deep with shredded native tree trimmings.
8) Water plantings with Garrett Juice, aerated compost tea, or other liquid organic fertilizer.

The purpose of preparing a natural organic bed is to build healthy soil that is alive with beneficial microbes that will provide natural fertility, protect natural plant systems, reduce watering needs, and reduce insect pests and disease pathogens.

For a little more detail:

Scrape away existing grass and weeds; add compost, lava sand, organic fertilizer, greensand, expanded shale, cornmeal, and dry molasses; and till into the native soil. Excavation of natural soil and additional ingredients such as concrete sand, peat moss, foreign soil, and pine bark should not be used. More compost is needed for shrubs and flowers than for ground cover. Add greensand to alkaline black-and-white soils (black clay on top of white rock) and high-calcium lime to acid soils. Decomposed granite and zeolite are effective for most soils.

Planting beds should be thoroughly moistened before planting begins. Do not plant dry plants or plant in dry soil. Shrubs and vines should be planted, after soaking the root balls, into moist, well-prepared beds and backfilled with the improved bed-preparation soil. Plants should be watered by sticking the hose down beside the root ball and soaking thoroughly.

Ground covers should be planted from 2 ¼" pots, 4" pots, or one-gallon containers. It is extremely important to dampen the soil prior to planting. In the hot months, this will greatly reduce plant losses. Consistent watering and mulching are also critical during the establishment period (first growing season). These small plants should be planted only in well-prepared moist beds.

AZALEAS, CAMELLIAS, GARDENIAS, AND RHODODENDRONS

Here is the plan for these higher-maintenance plants:

■ The best technique is to raise the entire bed. Second best is to

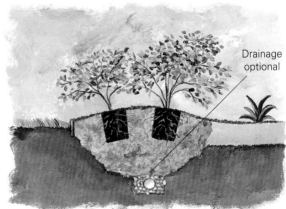

Azaleas, Camellias, Gardenias, and Rhododendrons

excavate and remove existing soil to a depth of 4". The width of the bed should be at least 24" for each row of plant.

■ Backfill with a mixture of 50% compost, 50% composted shredded tree trimmings, green sand, and lava sand @ 5 gallons each per cubic yard of mix. Place the mix in the bed area to a depth of 16". Be sure to thoroughly saturate this mixture in a tub or wheelbarrow prior to placing it in the bed.

■ Mound the beds so that the finished grade is about 12" above the adjacent grade.

■ Tear or cut pot-bound roots before planting. This is very important, for without this step, the roots will never break away from the ball and the plant often dies.

■ Soak root balls so they are sopping wet prior to planting in moist beds.

ANNUALS AND PERENNIALS

Flower beds should be built the same as shrub and ground-cover beds, but with the addition of 2 more inches of organic material. These beds should also be mounded or raised more than other plant beds if possible. Raised flower beds are critical for proper drainage.

■ **Flowers** (annuals & perennials) are often planted in the same beds as shrubs and ground covers. Some annuals and perennials can tolerate this, but gardeners would have greater success with their flowers if they would do one simple thing—raise or mound the flower beds. Flower beds can simply be mounded 6 to 9 inches by adding compost. Mixing at least some of the existing soil into the concoction is a good idea.

■ **Bulbs** should always be planted in prepared beds. Bulbs will do better with a tablespoon of rock phosphate cultivated into the bottom of the hole. Earthworm castings are an excellent addition to each bulb hole, and the plants will be larger and more showy if soaked in Garrett Juice or aerated compost tea.

TRANSPLANTING

Established plants should be relocated only during the dormant periods—usually in the fall or winter. The larger the plant, the more difficult the transplant. Smaller plants that have not developed an extensive root system can be moved during the growing season if watered in immediately. Transplanted plants should be installed with the same techniques used for new plants as explained previously.

MULCHING

Mulching should be done after planting is completed. Acceptable mulches are shredded hardwood bark, pine needles, coarse compost, pecan shells, or shredded native tree trimmings. Mulch should be at least 2" deep on top of planting beds; 3"–4" is better. Mulching helps hold moisture in the beds, controls weeds, and helps maintain proper soil temperatures. Do not pile mulch up onto the stems of plants.

Annual and Perennial Bed Preparation

Underground drainage. PVC pipe surrounded by gravel. Gravel only will often be enough.

Mounded bed

Raised bed with wall: use concrete or natural stone—never wood, especially treated wood that contains toxic chemicals. Railroad ties and CCA-treated wood should never be used.

Perennial Planting

1) Cut or tear pot-bound roots from the outside edge of the ball. 2) Dig a dish-shaped hole and set the plant so that the bottom is on firm existing soil and the top of the plant ball is slightly higher than the existing grade. 3) Backfill with the prepared bed soil. Settle the soil around the plant by watering slowly to remove all air pockets. Mulch bare soil, but do not allow mulch to pile up against the trunk of the plant.

Plant Sizes

Balled & burlapped   B & B   7–15 gal.   5 gal.   2–3 gal.   1 gal.   2 ¼–4" pots

Planting holes should be dug slightly less deep than the height of the earth ball. The top of the ball after watering should be slightly higher than the ground scale.

WEED CONTROL

Weed control is best done by hand and by mulching heavily. It's important to understand that a few weeds are not a big deal. Good cultural practices and healthy soil will eliminate most noxious weed problems. Spot spraying can be done with vinegar-based herbicides, such as soil-mender enhanced vinegar.

WILDFLOWERS

In the past, much of the wildflower planting was done by scattering the seed out over bare ground and hoping something would come up. As a result, few gardeners were having success with wildflowers. The proper method for growing wildflowers is as follows:

- Remove all weeds and loosen any heavily compacted areas. No need to remove rock. A light rototilling (1" deep) is the best bed preparation.
- Soil amendments and fertilizers are not needed other than a light application (5 lbs. per 1,000 sq. ft.) of 100% organic fertilizer.
- Treat the seed prior to planting with Garret Juice or aerated compost tea.
- Apply the seed at the recommended rate, making sure to get good soil–seed contact, and lightly rake the seed into the soil. Spring-blooming wildflowers should be planted the previous summer as Mother Nature does.
- Apply supplemental watering in the fall and in the spring if the weather is unseasonably dry. If rains are normal, no watering is needed.

GRASS PLANTING

Grass-planting techniques can be quite simple or can waste huge amounts of money. If you follow these simple techniques, your lawn establishment can be enjoyable and affordable.

- **Preparation** should include the removal of weed tops, debris, and rocks over 2" in diameter from the surface. Rocks within the soil are no problem because they actually aid positive drainage. Till to a depth of 1" and rake topsoil into a smooth grade. Deep rototilling is unnecessary and a waste of money unless the soil is heavily compacted.

  Add a thin layer (¼"–½") of compost. The addition of native topsoil isn't needed. Imported topsoil is a waste of money and can cause a perched (trapped) water table and lawn problems, unless there are low spots to be filled.

  Sloped areas should have an erosion protection material, such as jute mesh, placed on the soil prior to planting. Follow the manufacturer's recommendation for installation.

  Some people recommend and use herbicides to kill weeds prior to planting. I don't! These chemicals are hazardous and damaging to the soil biology.

- **Seeding and hydromulching** should be done so that the seed is in direct contact with the soil. The seed should be placed on the bare soil first and the hydromulch blown on top of the seed. One of the worst mistakes I see in grass planting is mixing the seed in the hydromulch. This causes the seed to germinate in the mulch, suspended above the soil, and many of the seeds are lost from drying out.

Night temperatures must be at least 65°–70° for Bermudagrass or centipede germination and no lower than 40° in the fall and winter for cool-season grasses.

After spreading the seed, thoroughly soak the ground and lightly water the seeded area 2–4 times per day. Fertilize with a 100% organic fertilizer sometime before the first mowing. As the seed germinates, watch for bare spots. Reseed these bare areas immediately. Continue the light watering until the grass has solidly covered the area. At this time, begin the regular watering and maintenance program.

- **Spot sodding** is done by planting 4" × 4" squares flush with the existing grade, 12" to 18" on center. Grading, smoothing, and leveling of the area to be grassed is important. Organic fertilizer should be applied after planting at the rate of 10 lbs. per 1,000 sq. ft. Regular maintenance and watering should be started at this time. This is not a planting procedure I recommend, because it is slow to cover, and often results in an uneven lawn.

- **Solid sod blocks** should be laid joint-to-joint after first applying lava sand at 80 lbs. per 1,000 sq. ft. Grading, leveling, and smoothing prior to planting is very important. The joints between the blocks of sod can be filled with compost to give an even more finished look to the lawn. *Thoroughly wet the top and bottom of each sod piece before planting. Roll the sod to remove air pockets. Apply ½" of compost on top of the new sod.*

- **Cool-season grasses** such as fescue, ryegrass, bentgrass, and bluegrass (*Poa trivialis*) should be planted in October, or anytime during the winter when the temperature is above 40°. In all cases, the newly applied seed should be watered at least twice daily until the grass has grown to the point of covering the ground.

INSTALLATION MISTAKES

Some of the worst installation mistakes I see on both residential and commercial projects are:

1. Failure to prepare and mulch beds properly.
2. Planting plants (especially trees) too low in the ground.
3. Failure to provide proper drainage.
4. Planting in smooth or glazed-wall holes.
5. Planting ill-adapted plant varieties.
6. Installing plants with dry root systems.
7. Staking and wrapping trees unnecessarily.

PLANT MAINTENANCE

UNLIKE BUILDINGS OR STRUCTURES, which look their best the day they are finished, gardens should look good when finished but improve each year. Landscaping, as opposed to architecture, is never static. Plants and gardens are complex living organisms that not only change seasonally but also grow and mature through time. The resulting change from the time of installation to later years is quite significant. The best maintenance program is one that is as natural as possible and works with the changes that are inevitable.

TREES

PROTECTION OF EXISTING TREES

Protection and maintenance of existing trees is a top priority. Staying away from trees' root systems and leaving grades and drainage patterns (both surface and underground) intact are essential to the health of trees. Although a tree's roots grow out far beyond the dripline of the foliage, protecting the area from the dripline to the trunk will give trees a pretty good chance to live. Installing a physical barrier such as a wire or wood fence is the only method that works to keep automobile and foot traffic, fill soil, and construction debris off the root system. Since buying new trees is expensive, I recommend you work hard to keep any existing ones alive and healthy. During construction on projects with trees, I highly recommend installing strong fences to block the workers from all parts of the site except where access can't be avoided. Also, the trees' root systems will greatly appreciate it if a thick layer of shredded native mulch is placed both inside and outside the fences. It is human nature to park, store materials, sit and have lunch, wash out equipment, and perform other activities in the shade of trees. Don't let them do it!

PRUNING

In general, people prune too much. I will admit that some trees require more pruning than others. For example, live oaks require more regular pruning than any other tree, whereas most other trees require almost no pruning other than the occasional removal of dead wood and limbs that are for some reason in the way.

Many trees are drastically thinned, artificially lifted, or severely cut back. A good rule of thumb for trimming trees is to try to copy Mother Nature's pruning techniques. Pruning a tree into an artificial shape is usually a waste of money, has ugly results, and is detrimental to the health of the plant. If you can't decide whether to trim or not, don't!

A common mistake is lifting or raising the bottom of the plant by removal of lower limbs. The lower limbs add to the grace and beauty of the tree, and the excessive removal of lower limbs can cause stress and lead to health-related problems. This procedure doesn't necessarily allow more light to the grass or other planting beneath. If the top of the tree has not been thinned, a solid canopy still exists and no significant increase of light to the ground plane has been created. It's best to remove only dead or damaged limbs, limbs that are rubbing, limbs with mistletoe or disease, and, in certain cases, enough of the canopy to allow shafts of sunlight all the way through the tree to the ground below.

Pruning cuts should never be made flush to the tree trunk. A stub, the branch collar, should be preserved because it is the part of the trunk that provides the natural healing process for the cut. It's better to err by leaving too much of a stub than to cut too close to the trunk. Flush cuts lead to decay and are a primary cause of cavities in trees.

I don't use or recommend pruning paint or wound dressing on pruning cuts. Damage to living tissue will always heal faster if exposed to fresh air. Pruning paint can seal moisture and disease spores into a protected environment and actually increase the spread of problems.

Cabling is another very expensive technique that in most cases is unnecessary and detrimental to the tree. Cabling simply moves the stress point from one position to another. Cables are unsightly and create an artificial tension in the tree that can actually lead to more wind and ice breakage instead of less. The only time cabling should be used is to keep a weak crotch from splitting. Never should cabling be used to hold up low-growing limbs.

AERATION

Mechanical aeration of the root systems of trees is done while aerating the lawn or planting beds under the trees. It should be done when the soil has been compacted or is dead from previous chemical use.

MULCHING

Trees should be mulched at the time of planting and at least for the first growing season. Place a 3"–4" layer of mulch over the root ball of the tree to prevent the competition of grass roots. If trees are planted in beds, the entire bed should be mulched. The mulch should slope from its deepest at the outside edge of the hole to 0" at the tree trunk. Mulch should never be piled on the trunks of trees. As of this writing, Houston holds the distinction of being the worst tree-mulching city in the United States, maybe in the world. Whoever started the insane procedure of building "volcanoes" of mulch at the bases of trees should be sentenced to the job of removing all of these detrimental piles from all the trees in Greater Houston. It will be a life sentence—there are a bunch of them.

FERTILIZING

The rate of fertilizer should be based on the surface area to be fertilized rather than on the caliper inches of the tree trunk. Organic programs feed the soil rather than the plants, so the amount of fertilizer is related to the amount of area, not the number, kind, or size of plants.

I normally fertilize once in the early spring and again in early summer with a

EARTHWORMS ARE NATURE'S TILLERS AND SOIL CONDITIONERS. BESIDES INTEGRATING ORGANIC MATERIAL INTO THE SOIL, EARTHWORMS MANUFACTURE GREAT FERTILIZER. ONE REASON FOR USING NATURAL FERTILIZERS IN YOUR GARDEN IS THAT THEY ENCOURAGE NATIVE EARTHWORMS.

100% organic fertilizer at the rate of 20 lbs. per 1,000 sq. ft. A third application is sometimes needed in the fall. Fertilizer should be spread on the surface of the soil rather than put in holes around the trees. The root system of trees is shallower than most people realize; at least 85% of the roots are located in the top 6" of soil. Fertilizing the entire property is the best way to feed trees. And of course, synthetic high-nitrogen salt-based fertilizers should never be used around trees.

WATERING

Watering is the most variable function in the maintenance puzzle due to variable soils, weather, plant materials, and plant exposure to sun or shade.

If trees are planted properly in the beginning, very little extra watering is needed except during the heat of the summer. The best watering philosophy is to water heavily and deeply, then to wait as long as possible before watering again—within reason of course.

Newly planted trees should be thoroughly soaked every other week in the hot growing season and once a month in the cooler seasons. This watering should be done in addition to regular watering of the grass areas or planting areas surrounding the trees. Obviously, rain will alter this schedule. Once trees are established, a regular watering of the surrounding planting areas should be enough. During periods of extreme drought, the soaking procedure may need to be used again.

PEST CONTROL

Adapted plants growing in healthy soil have a powerful built-in immunity to insect pests and diseases. For the limited pest problems that pop up, here are the basics.

Spraying for insects and diseases on a preventative basis wastes money, adds unnecessarily to the chemicals in our environment, and kills more beneficials than the targeted pests. Use compost tea, seaweed, molasses, and natural vinegar as a general spray control. It works by stimulating the beneficials. Sprays for insects and diseases should be applied only after pests are seen. Biological controls should be the first choice because they work best in the long run and don't hurt the beneficial insects and microorganisms. Aphids, for example, can be controlled with a strong blast of water and the release of ladybugs. Beneficial insects should be put out at dusk after wetting all the foliage. Fire ants can be controlled with beneficial nematodes, plant oil products, or cinnamon dusted on mounds.

Bacillus thuringiensis (Bt) is a biological control for cutworms, loopers, and caterpillars, but it will also kill butterflies, so use rarely and carefully. Ladybugs, green lacewings, and trichogramma wasps provide excellent control of aphids, caterpillars, spider mites, worms, and other small insects. Garlic-pepper tea, orange oil, and other plant-oil products can be used for general pest control. Plant Wash is another excellent general insect preventer and even better for disease control. More details can be found in the *Texas Bug Book*.

Harsh chemical pesticides will probably continue to be used, but if just some of you gardeners elect to use some of the natural alternatives, we will have made a step in the right direction. Besides being extremely dangerous and harmful to people and pets, strong chemicals also kill the beneficial microorganisms, earthworms, insects, lizards, frogs, and birds.

WEED CONTROL

Herbicide application under any tree is risky and should be avoided. Improvement of soil health, hand removal, and mulch on all bare soil is all that is usually needed. The exceptions are corn gluten meal, vinegar-based sprays, and other natural weed controls.

SICK TREE TREATMENT

Oak Wilt Control

Texas A&M and the Texas Forest Service recommend a program of trenching to separate the roots of sick trees from those of healthy trees, cutting down sick and nearby healthy trees, and injecting a toxic chemical fungicide called Alamo directly into the trunks or root flares of the trees. I don't recommend this program because it does nothing to address the cause of the disease.

Trees succumb to insect pests and diseases because they are in stress and sick. Mother Nature then sends in the cleanup crews. The insects and pathogens are just doing their job—trying to take out the unfit plants. Most sickness is environmental—too much water, not enough water, too much fertilizer, wrong kind of fertilizer, toxic chemical pesticides, compaction of soil, grade changes, ill-adapted plant varieties, and/or overplanting single plant species and creating monocultures, such as American elms in the Northwest and red oak/live oak communities in certain parts of Texas.

My plan is simple. Keep trees in a healthy condition so their immune systems can resist insect pests and diseases. It has been noticed by many farmers and ranchers that oak wilt doesn't bother some trees—especially those that are mulched and those where the natural habitat under the trees has been maintained.

For trees that are infested with oak wilt or any other disease, I recommend the procedure called the *Sick Tree Treatment* as explained below.

Step 1: Remove Excess Soil from above the Root Ball

A very high percentage of trees have been planted too low or have had fill soil or eroded soil added on top of the root flare and roots. Soil on top of the root ball reduces oxygen availability and leads to circling and girdling roots. Soil, or even heavy mulch, on trunks keeps the bark constantly moist, which can rot or girdle trees. Many new trees are too low in their containers. Excess soil and circling and girdling roots should be removed before planting. Removing soil from the root flares of trees should be done professionally with a tool called an Air Spade. Homeowners can do the work by hand with a stiff brush and Shop Vac if the soil has the proper moisture.

Step 2: Aerate the Root Zone Heavily

Don't rip, till, or plow the soil. That destroys all the feeder roots. Punch holes (with core aerators or ag devices such as the Air-Way) heavily throughout the root zone. Start between the dripline and the trunk and go far out beyond the dripline. Holes 6"–8" deep are ideal, but any depth is beneficial. An alternative is to spray the root zone with a living organism product or biostimulant such as an aerated compost tea.

Step 3: Apply Organic Amendments

Apply Texas greensand at about 40–80 lbs. per 1,000 sq. ft., lava sand at about 80–120 lbs. per 1,000 sq. ft., horticultural cornmeal at about 20–30 lbs. per 1,000 sq. ft., and dry molasses at about 10–20 lbs. per 1,000 sq. ft. Cornmeal is a natural disease fighter, and molasses is a carbohydrate source to feed the microbes in the soil. Expanded shale applied in a ½" layer is also very helpful if the budget allows this step. Apply a 1" layer of compost followed by a 3" layer of shredded native tree trimmings; however, do not pile up mulch on the root flare or the trunk. In turf, use a 1" layer of quality compost. Smaller amounts of these materials can be used where budget restrictions exist.

Step 4: Spray Trees and Soil

Spray the ground, trunks, limbs, twigs, and foliage of trees with compost tea or the entire Garrett Juice mixture (see formula in the "Watering" section for "Annuals, Perennials, and Herbs"). Do this monthly or more often if possible. For large-scale farms and ranches, a one-time spraying is beneficial if the budget doesn't allow ongoing sprays. Adding garlic tea or cornmeal juice to the spray is also beneficial for disease control while the tree is in trouble. Cornmeal juice is a natural fungal control that is made by soaking horticultural or whole ground cornmeal in water at one cup per 5 gallons of water. Screen out the solids and spray without further dilution. Cornmeal juice can be mixed with compost tea, Garrett Juice, or any other natural foliar-feeding spray. It can also be used as a soil drench for the control of soil-borne diseases. Dry granulated garlic can also be used on the soil in the root zone at about 1–2 lbs. per 1,000 sq. ft. for additional disease control.

Step 5: Stop Using High-Nitrogen Fertilizers and Toxic Chemical Pesticides

Toxic chemical pesticides kill beneficial nematodes, other helpful microbes, and the good insects. They also control the pest insects poorly. Synthetic fertilizers are harsh; high in salt; often contaminated; and destructive to the chemistry, the structure, and the life in the soil. They also feed plants poorly.

P.S.: During drought conditions, adding soil moisture is a critical component.

SHRUBS

PRUNING

No pruning is required at the time of planting, and yearly pruning should be kept to a minimum, leaving the plants as soft and natural as possible. Pick-pruning of shrubs, although somewhat time-consuming, has always been my favorite method. Due to time constraints, a combination of light shearing and careful pick-pruning will create the best effect. Severe shearing or boxing should be avoided except in extremely formal gardens. Flowering shrubs, especially spring bloomers, need to be pruned immediately after flowering, not later in the season, so that no damage will be done to stems forming the buds for the next year's flower display.

MULCHING

Shrubs should be mulched at the time of planting. The mulch does an excellent job of holding moisture in the soil, preventing weeds, and keeping the ground cool, thus aiding in the quick establishment of root systems.

FERTILIZING

Shrubs should be fertilized the same as trees: in the early spring, again in early to midsummer, and a third time in the fall if the soil still needs improvement. As with trees, I recommend fertilizing the ground surface at the rate of 20 lbs. per 1,000 sq. ft. using a 100% organic fertilizer. Avoid a concentration of fertilizer at the trunk or main stem of the plant. A thorough watering following any application of fertilizers is best, but not critical with natural organic fertilizers.

WATERING

I recommend the same watering technique for shrubs as for trees. However, since the plants are smaller in size, they can dry out faster, so a little more care is needed in monitoring the watering program. I recommend a sprinkler system unless you have an awful lot of free time to stand around at the end of a water hose. Above-ground bubblers and soaker hoses are OK, but I would avoid below-ground drip systems. All drip systems need to be monitored closely because they can fail and cause dry and/or super wet spots.

PEST CONTROL

I recommend the same techniques for shrubs as explained previously for trees. Remember that effective pest control is greatly enhanced by keeping your plants as healthy as possible using 100% organic fertilizers and generous amounts of well-made compost. Insects and diseases primarily attack weak, unhealthy, stressed plants. Also remember that it's not necessary to kill every bad bug in your garden—a few are no problem and are an important part of Nature's systems. A healthy population of beneficial insects is the best control.

Diseases can be controlled with garlic tea sprays, dry granulated garlic, whole ground cornmeal, cornmeal juice sprays, or commercial products like Plant Wash.

WEED CONTROL

Pull the weeds by hand and mulch heavily. Spot spray with vinegar-based herbicide.

GROUND COVERS AND VINES

PRUNING

No pruning is required at planting time. The only regular ground-cover pruning I recommend, other than edging as needed, is a one-time late-winter or early-spring mowing with a lawnmower set on its highest setting. Most ground covers used in large areas other than English ivy can be mowed, saving a lot of time and money.

To prevent tearing the plants, sharpen the blades of the lawnmower and, if mowing large areas, stop occasionally to resharpen.

Vines should be kept trimmed back to the desired size and can be trimmed at any time. Prune flowering vines immediately after the plant has stopped blooming. Pruning at other times can eliminate the next year's flower production.

MULCHING

Mulching bare areas should be done after the plants have been installed. Once the plants are established, mulching is generally not needed because the foliage takes over that function, but remulching should be done if any bare areas appear during the season.

FERTILIZING

The fertilization I recommend for ground covers and vines is the same as for shrubs. Remember that 100% organic fertilizers will give you the best results in the long run.

WATERING

During the establishment period of ground cover, supplemental watering is usually needed in addition to the sprinkler system because the very small root systems of ground covers can dry out quickly. The key to the quick establishment of ground cover is keeping the soil evenly moist, not sopping wet. Mulch will help greatly in this regard.

PEST CONTROL

Use the same organic techniques for ground cover and vines as mentioned previously for trees and shrubs. Diseases can be controlled with garlic tea sprays, dry granulated garlic, whole ground cornmeal, and cornmeal juice sprays.

ANNUALS, PERENNIALS, AND HERBS

PRUNING

Spent flowers and stems should be removed as they fade in order to encourage new blooms. Plants that have become damaged or diseased should be removed.

MULCHING

Mulching the exposed soil around the plants should be done at planting, and remulching should be done as any bare areas appear during the season.

FERTILIZING

Annuals and perennials should be fertilized, along with the trees, shrubs, and lawns, with 100% organic fertilizers. For additional flower production, use earthworm castings at 10 lbs. per 1,000 sq. ft. and bat guano at 10 lbs. per 1,000 sq. ft. in addition to the basic fertilization. Spray the plants and drench the soil at least twice per month with Garrett Juice or aerated compost tea. There are now micronized products available that give even faster results. Potted plants should be fertilized every 2 to 3 weeks with the following mixture. Per gallon of water: 1–2 cups manure compost tea, 1 tablespoon liquid seaweed, 1 tablespoon natural apple cider vinegar, 1 tablespoon blackstrap molasses. This mix is now called Garrett Juice and is also used for foliar feeding and soil drenches.

WATERING

Water as needed to maintain an even moisture level. Beds should never be soggy wet or bone dry. Occasional deep watering is much better than frequent sprinkles. Potted plants and new beds should be watered daily through hot months and as needed during the cooler months. Once the plants have filled in solidly, use the same watering schedule as for the rest of the garden, but check the pots often.

PEST CONTROL

Use the same technique as explained earlier for trees. Special exceptions are covered at each specific plant in the pages that follow. Plant-oil sprays do an excellent job of controlling pest insects. *Bacillus thuringiensis* controls cutworms, loopers, and other caterpillars. Keeping the soil healthy and nutritious by using generous amounts of compost will help keep pests to a minimum. Insects and diseases primarily prey on unhealthy, stressed plants. Don't forget to release ladybugs, praying mantids, and green lacewings. Wasps, bees, dragonflies, fireflies, and assassin bugs are also beneficial garden insects.

Certain plants do a good job of repelling insects. The best are artemisia, basil, lavender, pennyroyal mint, rosemary, sage, garlic, santolina, lemon balm, and thyme.

Diseases can be controlled with garlic tea sprays, dry granulated garlic, whole ground cornmeal, and cornmeal juice sprays. The latest commercial product is called Plant Wash.

WEED CONTROL

I prefer hand pulling and mulch. Straight vinegar, 100 grain (10% acid) or stronger, is a good nonselective herbicide for hot-weather weeds. Into the vinegar add 1 oz. orange oil, 1 tablespoon molasses, and 1 teaspoon soap. The commercial product is Soil Mender Enhanced Vinegar.

GENERAL GUIDELINE: WATER AS NEEDED—AND NO MORE.

GRASS

MOWING

Maintenance of grass is the most time-consuming and expensive part of garden maintenance. Start by using the kind of grass that is most appropriate for your property. Mowing should be done on a regular basis and the clippings should be left on the lawn. No more than a third of the leaf blades should be removed in any one mowing. Mow grass according to the following guidelines:

- Bermudagrass, St. Augustine, and centipede—2"–3" height—once a week
- Tifgrasses—½"–¾" height—twice a week
- Zoysiagrass—3"–4" height—every other week
- Buffalograss—3"–8" height—monthly or less often

Scalping should never be done except before planting additional seed.

FERTILIZING

Fertilization of grass can be handled in exactly the same manner as described above for trees and shrubs. In fact, the easiest and most cost-effective technique is to fertilize everything in your garden at the same time. Never use chemical weed-and-feed fertilizers. They are very dangerous. The "weed" part of the name refers to herbicides that kill plants. You should also avoid the often-recommended high-nitrogen synthetic fertilizers. The overuse of inorganic fertilizers contaminates the soil and water systems with salt and cancer-causing nitrates. Organic fertilizers have lower levels of nitrogen and are naturally slow release. They have excellent buffering abilities and provide organic material to build the humus in the soil.

WATERING

Again, watering is the most variable part of the puzzle and should be applied only when necessary rather than on a calendar schedule. Occasional deep watering is better than light sprinkles on a more regular basis. The amount of water to be used will vary tremendously from one site to the next, depending on the soils, sun exposure, location, and how green you want your grass. Consistency is the key. Once your soil is organic and healthy, less irrigation will be needed.

Establish a level of moisture that you think is appropriate, one that isn't too wet or too dry, and stick with that program. If you have a sprinkler system, turn it on manually whenever water is needed.

Obviously, rain, cloudy days, snow, wind, drainage, type of watering, amount of water per time, and water bills all affect your watering program. It would be ideal to get to a point of watering no more than once per week.

Water-Saving Tips

- Repair leaky faucets.
- Use a nozzle or spray gun on the hose so water can be shut off when not in use.
- Use a broom, not a hose, to clean paving surfaces.
- Collect rainfall in containers to use for landscape or pot plant watering.
- Put grass and planting beds on different sections of the sprinkler system when possible.
- Run sprinkler system manually when needed rather than on a set schedule.
- Water during the cooler parts of the day to reduce evaporation.
- Avoid watering when windy, if possible.

AERATION

Lack of oxygen is often the most limiting factor in the soil. Aeration is an important and often-overlooked technique. To aerate grass areas, simply punch holes in the ground with any kind of equipment available in your area. Landscape contractors can be hired to do the work. It is amazing what this simple procedure can produce. Grass will green up as if fertilization has been done, and the root systems of nearby shrubs and trees will appreciate the introduction of oxygen into the soil. Be sure to mark the location of the sprinkler heads to avoid damage. This procedure is only necessary the first year or when compaction of the soil has been done.

PEST CONTROL

Lawns rarely have insect problems if the soil is healthy and drains well. Diseases can be controlled with garlic tea sprays, dry granulated garlic, whole ground cornmeal, and cornmeal juice sprays.

MAINTENANCE MISTAKES

There are many incorrect and unnecessary maintenance procedures. Some of the worst mistakes are as follows:

1. Building volcanoes of mulch at the base of trees.
2. Spreading sand or loam on lawns in the spring.
3. Topping or dehorning trees.
4. Installing steel curbing at the edge of beds at sidewalks or other paving surfaces instead of properly lowering the grade of the edge of the bed.
5. Overtrimming trees and shrubs.
6. Using "weed-and-feed" fertilizers.
7. Using toxic chemical products in general.
8. Not removing sick or overgrown plants.
9. Using synthetic high-nitrogen salt-based fertilizers.

MAINTENANCE BY THE CALENDAR

JANUARY

Plant

- Cold-hardy transplants outdoors.
- Spring flowers and vegetable seeds indoors for later transplanting.
- Fruit and pecan trees, asparagus, berries, English peas, grapes, onions, beets, and Irish potatoes.
- Shrubs, vines, balled-and-burlapped or containerized trees.
- Complete bulb planting by early January. "Force" bulbs in pots indoors. Paperwhites are the easiest to grow.
- Transplant plants during this dormant period.

Fertilize

- Cool-season flowering plants.
- Asparagus beds in late January with organic fertilizer and compost.
- Cool-season grasses at ½ rate, about 10 lbs. per 1,000 sq. ft.
- Drench Garrett Juice as a root stimulator for new shrubs and trees monthly until established.

Prune

- Shade trees by removing dead, damaged, and out-of-place limbs, water sprouts, and ground shoots.
- Summer-flowering trees as necessary to control form.
- Evergreen shrubs lightly if needed.
- Fruit trees and grapes. However, the best time is just before bud break in late winter.
- Remove all vines from trees and pull ground covers back from the base of trees.
- DO NOT prune the tops of crape myrtles.
- Do not make flush cuts and do not use pruning paint.

Water

- Potted plants.
- Spot-water any dry areas to avoid plant desiccation.

Pest Control

- Spray dormant turf with vinegar-based herbicide for cool-season weeds. Do not use acetic acid products. Use real vinegar made from grain alcohol.
- Spray horticultural oil if needed on scale-prone plants such as camellias, hollies, oaks, and pecan and fruit trees. Remember that this organic pesticide kills good bugs as well as pests.
- Spray houseplants with plant-oil products or Lemon Joy liquid soap at 1 teaspoon per gallon of water to combat mealybugs, spider mites, and scale. Apply horticultural cornmeal and coffee grounds to the soil.

Odd Jobs

- Cover tender plants with floating row cover during extreme cold.
- Have soil tests run at Texas Plant & Soil Lab. Do not use the A&M service or any other labs that do not give information on what nutrients are available to plants.
- Turn compost pile monthly or more often and keep moist. There is no reason to try to keep it warm with coverings or sunlight. The compost action is down in the center of the pile.
- Plan spring landscape improvement projects and begin construction activities.
- Prepare garden soil by adding compost and volcanic rock powders and mulching bare soil. Take mowers, tillers, and trimmers into shop for repairs before spring.
- Don't forget to feed the birds!

FEBRUARY

Plant

- Trees, shrubs, ground covers, vines, and hardy perennials such as roses.
- Asparagus, broccoli, Brussels sprouts, cabbage, carrots, cauliflower, English peas, onions, potatoes, Swiss chard, other cold-tolerant vegetables, and strawberries for harvest next spring.
- Cool-season annuals and those that can take some cool weather, such as ageratum, alyssum, cockscomb, coreopsis, cosmos, nasturtium, petunia, phlox, and salvia.
- Fruit trees, grapes, pecans, and berries.
- Summer-blooming bulbs such as amaryllis, canna, and gladiola.
- Transplant existing landscape plants before the new spring growth begins. Do not trim to thin the plants;

the idea that it compensates for root loss is nonsense.

■ Divide and transplant crowded summer- and fall-blooming perennials as needed.

Fertilize

■ All planting areas and turf with a natural organic fertilizer at approximately 20 lbs. per 1,000 sq. ft. in the **first major fertilization of the year.** If the soil is already healthy, the rate can be reduced to 10 lbs. per 1,000 sq. ft. For pre-emergent weed control and fertilizer, apply corn gluten meal at 20 lbs. per 1,000 sq. ft.

■ Cool-season flowers with earthworm castings, fish meal, bat guano, or organic fertilizer such as Yum Yum Mix at 10–20 lbs. per 1,000 sq. ft.

■ Spray growing plants with Garrett Juice and/or aerated compost tea. Drench root zone of newly planted or transplanted plants.

■ Avoid all synthetic fertilizers but especially the weed-and-feed types that contain herbicides that will kill your trees. Scotts Bonus S is the worst.

Prune

■ Shade and ornamental trees lightly (if necessary) to remove dead, diseased, and crossing limbs. Remove limbs either because they are in the way or to allow more light to reach ground plants. Do not thin out trees for no reason.

■ Peaches and plums by 40%–50% to encourage growth at a 45° angle; grapes, by 80%–90%; other fruit trees as needed. Pecans need little to no pruning. Do not prune crape myrtles other than to remove ground sprouts.

■ Evergreens and summer-flowering plants if necessary. Remove the longest shoots to reduce height and protect the natural shapes of plants.

■ Bush-form roses. Climbers and roses that bloom only once should be pruned after their primary flowering has ended.

■ Winter-damaged foliage from liriope, ophiopogon, Asian jasmine, and other ground covers. Asian jasmine can be mowed to maintain low neat appearance.

■ Remove ground covers from bases of trees to expose the soil and root flares. Remove soil from root flares if needed. Homeowners can do the work with water and shop vacs or with a stiff brush if the soil is moist.

■ Remove invasive plants such as privet, Japanese honeysuckle, briars, and poison ivy.

Water

■ Winter annuals and any other dry-soil areas as needed. Turf areas should be watered every few weeks during drought weather.

Pest Control

■ Giant bark aphids need no treatment in most cases.

■ Horticultural oil can be sprayed for serious infestations of scale insects. Be sure to keep mixture shaken while using, and follow label instructions carefully. Use sparingly if at all. Oil kills beneficials as well as pests.

■ If needed, apply beneficial nematodes to help control grub worms, fleas, fire ants, and other pests. Remember that most grubs found in the garden are beneficial. They feed on dead organic matter rather than on plant roots.

■ Start the Organic Fruit and Pecan Tree Program at the "pink bud" stage. See the home page of dirtdoctor.com for a printout of the most current program.

Odd Jobs

■ Adjust and repair sprinkler system. Work on drainage problems.

■ Have soil tested with a lab that offers organic recommendations. Watch for accumulations of any single elements.

■ Have maintenance equipment repaired for spring use.

■ Sharpen hoes, pruning tools, and mower blades.

■ Add compost and top-dressing mulch to all bare-soil areas. Also add to any unhealthy-looking plants.

■ Turn the compost pile regularly. Add moisture during dry weather.

■ Do not scalp the lawn. Do not catch grass clippings.

■ Feed and water the birds!

MARCH

Plant

■ Trees, shrubs, and other permanent plants.

■ Warm-season crops such as black-eyed peas, okra, peppers, squash, tomatoes, etc. Plant a mixture of varieties and include some open-pollinated choices after last killing-freeze date—your guess is as good as mine.

■ Summer herbs: lavender, lemongrass, lemon verbena, mint, oregano, sage, salad burnet, thyme, etc.

■ Continue to plant cool-season annuals. Begin planting warm-season types.

Fertilize

- All planting areas with a natural organic fertilizer at approximately 20 lbs. per 1,000 sq. ft. (if not done in February).
- Spray all growing plants with Garrett Juice.
- Drench the roots of newly planted plants with Garrett Juice and mycorrhizal fungi products.

Prune

- Spring-flowering shrubs and vines only after they finish blooming.
- Fruit trees just before bud break if not already done.
- Finish major pruning if necessary—no flush cuts.

Water

- Annuals and all dry soil areas as needed.
- Potted plants as necessary.
- Wildflower areas in dry years.
- Turf during drought conditions.

Pest Control

- Don't use any toxic chemical pesticides.
- Loopers and caterpillars: Spray *Bacillus thuringiensis* (Bt) biological worm spray. Add one ounce of molasses per gallon of spray. Release trichogramma wasps.
- Pillbugs, slugs, snails: Spray garlic-pepper tea and dust around plants with a mix of hot pepper, natural diatomaceous earth, and cedar flakes. Spray plant-oil products for serious infestations.
- Aphids: Use a blast of water and a release of ladybugs. Add 2 ounces molasses per gallon of water for better results.
- Black spot, powdery mildew, and bacterial leaf spot: Spray Garrett Juice plus a cup of spray Plant Wash per gallon of spray or spray cornmeal juice.
- Sycamore anthracnose: Spray cornmeal juice or 3% hydrogen peroxide as leaves emerge and apply the entire Sick Tree Treatment.
- Fruit trees: Spray Garrett Juice plus garlic tea at pink bud and again after flowers have fallen from the trees. Spray Garrett Juice only every two weeks. See the Organic Fruit and Pecan Tree Program (at dirtdoctor.com) for more details.

Odd Jobs

- Turn the compost pile and keep it moist.

- Use completed compost for bed preparation—use partially completed compost or shredded native tree trimmings as top-dressing mulch.
- Mulch all bare soil but do not pile mulch on the stems of plants.
- Don't ever bag the clippings.
- Feed and water the birds!

APRIL

Plant

- Turf grass from plugs, solid sod, sprigs, or seed.
- Roses and other shrubs if not done earlier.
- Fruit and pecan trees.
- Warm-season flowers, including (for sun) begonia, copper leaf, cosmos, lantana, marigold, periwinkle, portulaca, zinnia; (for shade) begonia, caladium, coleus, impatiens, and nicotiana.
- Tropical plants.
- Summer herbs.
- Continue to plant warm-season vegetables, including beans, corn, cucumbers, eggplant, melons, okra, southern peas, squash, sweet potatoes, and tomatoes.
- Summer- and fall-flowering perennials.
- Herb-garden plants in beds, pots, and hanging baskets.

Fertilize

- Summer-flowering shrubs and roses.
- Spray all plant foliage with aerated compost tea or Garrett Juice. Add garlic tea if minor insect or disease problems exist. Add Plant Wash for diseases.
- Apply Garrett Juice monthly to the soil as a root stimulator around newly planted trees and shrubs.
- Treat chlorotic plants with Texas greensand or the entire Sick Tree Treatment.

Prune

- Spring-blooming vines and shrubs, such as azalea, flowering quince, forsythia, and spirea, immediately after bloom.
- Fall asters, Mexican bush sage, mums, and other fall-blooming perennials.
- Spent blooms from roses.
- Pick-prune hedges (or lightly shear them if you must) to be wider at the bottom of the plant for better light and thicker growth.
- Thin peach fruit to 5" apart, plums to 4" apart, apples and pears to 1 per cluster.

Water

- All planting areas deeply but infrequently during dry periods.
- Potted plants as needed. Add 2 oz. Garrett Juice and/or 1 cup aerated compost tea per gallon of water.

Pest Control

- Do not spray roses with toxic chemicals.
- Release green lacewings for control of thrips in roses, glads, or other flowers.
- Snails, slugs, pillbugs: Spray garlic-pepper tea, or dust around plants with cedar flakes, hot pepper, and natural diatomaceous earth. Mulch plants with pine needles. Spray plant-oil products if necessary.
- Release trichogramma wasps for pecan casebearers and other caterpillar pests.
- Ticks, fleas, and chiggers: Apply natural diatomaceous earth when weather is dry and beneficial nematodes anytime. Spray plant-oil products if necessary.
- Treat peaches and plums and other fruit with the Organic Fruit and Pecan Tree Program. The latest version is on the home page of dirtdoctor.com.
- Aphids: Spray a water blast and release ladybugs. Add 1–2 oz. of molasses for better results.
- Black spot on roses: Spray Garrett Juice plus garlic tea. See Rose Program on home page of dirtdoctor.com. Also use plant wash spray.
- Fire Ants: Apply beneficial nematodes. Treat mounds with Spinosad or drench with a mound-drench mixture of orange oil, molasses, and compost tea. Applying dry molasses or cinnamon is also effective.
- Remove the plant stress that brought on the pests in the first place, or they will be back.

Odd Jobs

- Mow weekly and leave clippings on the lawn.
- Turn compost pile.
- Continue to add new vegetative matter and manure to existing and additional compost piles.
- Mulch all bare soil.
- Feed and water the birds!

MAY

Plant

- All warm-season lawn grasses from plugs, sod, seed, or sprigs or by hydromulching. Zoysia should only be planted in solid soil. Also plant the tall prairie grasses from seed, including big and little bluestem, Indiangrass, switchgrass, sideoats grama, eastern gama, etc.
- Tropical color in beds or pots, including allamanda, bougainvillea, hibiscus, mandevilla, penta, and others.
- All trees and shrubs from containers. Hardened-off balled-and-burlapped plants also.
- Warm-season annual color plants: begonia, caladium, cosmos, impatiens, lantana, periwinkle, verbena, zinnia, and others.
- Perennials, including asters, cannas, glads, summer bulbs, mums, and other fall perennials.
- Ground covers, including Asian jasmine, English ivy, horseherb, liriope, ophiopogon, Persian ivy, and purple wintercreeper from 1 ¼" to 4" pots.
- Hot-weather vegetables, including melons, okra, peppers, southern peas, and squash.

Fertilize

- All annual flowers and potted plants with organic fertilizers such as Yum Yum Mix or Nature's Creation. Spray Garrett Juice or spread aerated compost on all foliage every two weeks, or as time and budget allow. Drench root zones of plants for root stimulation with Garrett Juice.

Prune

- Climbing roses—after their bloom.
- Spring-flowering shrubs, vines, and trees after they have bloomed.
- Pinch away the growing tips of mums weekly.

Water

- All planting areas deeply but infrequently during dry periods.
- Potted plants regularly. Add Garrett Juice or aerated compost tea.

Pest Control

- Spray troublesome insect pests with plant oil products and diseases like powdery mildew with Plant Wash. Do not use toxic chemicals.
- Continue to release trichogramma wasps for pecan casebearers and troublesome caterpillars.
- Fleas and ticks: Apply natural diatomaceous earth in dry weather and beneficial nematodes anytime.

For chiggers, apply elemental sulfur at 4 lbs. per 1,000 sq. ft. or less, or spray with mound-drench products or other plant-oil products.

- Cabbage loopers and other caterpillars: Release trichogramma wasps and, as a last resort, spray *Bacillus thuringiensis* (Bt) or the Liquid Fire Ant Control formula (available at dirtdoctor.com). Add one ounce of molasses per gallon of Bt spray.
- Aphids on tender new growth: Spray a strong water blast and release ladybugs.
- Release green lacewings and ladybugs for general control.
- Lacebugs on azaleas, sycamores: Spray garlic-pepper tea or Plant Wash with one of the orange-oil mound-drench products.
- Mosquitoes: Mist or spray plant-oil products and apply minced or granulated garlic to site and to potted plants.
- Brown patch or other fungal diseases: Apply horticultural or whole ground cornmeal at 10–20 lbs. per 1,000 sq. ft. Spray and/or drench soil with garlic tea.
- Weeds: Hand remove or use mechanical devices. Spot-spray with vinegar-based products. Formulas are on dirtdoctor.com. The commercial product is Soil Mender's Enhanced Vinegar.

Odd Jobs

- Mow weekly and leave clippings on the lawn.
- Turn compost pile and continue to add new ingredients.
- Mulch all bare soil with shredded trimmings from your own property or shredded cedar.
- Don't forget to feed and water the birds!

JUNE

Plant

- All warm-season grasses: Bermuda, zoysia, and St. Augustine by solid sod; Bermuda and buffalo grasses and other native grasses by seed.
- Summer annual and perennial color: amaranth, pride of Barbados, begonia, caladium, coleus, copperleaf, cosmos, esperanza, gomphrena, lantana, marigold, periwinkle, purslane, portulaca, zinnia, and various tropicals, such as cockscomb, cosmos, hardy hibiscus, salvia, and more.
- Warm-season food crops: amaranth, Malabar spinach,

okra, pumpkins, southern peas, squash, and sweet potatoes.
- Tropical color: bougainvillea, hibiscus, ixora, firebush, penta, allamanda, mandevilla, etc.
- Shrubs and trees, especially summer-flowering varieties like crape myrtle, so you can see the flower color.
- Fall tomatoes and other fall vegetable crops.

Fertilize

- All planting areas with organic fertilizer. This should be the **second major fertilization of the year.** Use about 20 lbs. of fertilizer per 1,000 sq. ft. To give plants an extra boost, use fish meal or corn gluten meal.
- Spray all plantings and lawns with Garrett Juice every two weeks or at least once a month.
- Iron and general trace mineral deficiency results in yellowed leaves with dark green veins on the youngest growth. Drench soil with Garrett Juice and Texas greensand. Magnesium products will also help. Use high-calcium lime for calcium deficiency.
- Apply the Sick Tree Treatment to any ailing trees and other woody plants.
- Avoid all synthetic fertilizers, especially nitrogen-only products like 24-0-0.

Prune

- Long, erratic shoots from abelia, elaeagnus, Lady Banks roses, etc.
- Blackberries to remove fruiting canes after harvest. Prune new canes to 3' in height to encourage side branching.
- Dead and damaged wood from trees and shrubs as needed.
- Remove spent blooms and shear by one-third flowering plants that have started to decline. Don't wait until they have completely stopped blooming.

Water

- All planting areas deeply but infrequently during dry periods.
- Potted plants regularly. Daily watering is needed for some plants. Add 2 ounces of Garrett Juice per gallon of water at least once a month.

Pest Control

- Spray Plant Wash on problem insects and diseases.
- Yellow lower leaves on tomatoes: Spray garlic

tea and/or cornmeal juice with compost tea.

- Spider mites: Spray Garrett Juice or any seaweed product as needed. Add Plant Wash for more effect.
- Fleas, ticks, chiggers: Dust with natural diatomaceous earth in dry weather and release beneficial nematodes anytime.
- Gray leaf spot: Reduce fertilizers and spray garlic tea and/or cornmeal juice with Garrett Juice.
- Bagworms and other caterpillars: Release trichogramma wasps and spray if needed with *Bacillus thuringiensis* (Bt). Spinosad and mound-drench products containing orange oil can also be used. Garrett Juice plus 2 ounces of orange oil per gallon of spray is also effective.
- Scale insects, including mealybugs: Spray plant-oil products or mound-drench products.
- Black spot on roses, mildew, and other fungi: Spray Garrett Juice plus garlic tea or diluted milk and drench the soil with garlic tea or apply dry granulated garlic. See dirtdoctor.com home page for the entire Organic Rose Program.
- Weeds: Hand remove and work on improving soil health. Spot-spray vinegar-based products.
- Lacebugs, elm leaf beetles, green June bugs, etc.: Spray garlic-pepper tea, horticultural oil, plant-oil products, or mound-drench products containing orange oil. Spinosad products will also work on this and other insect pests.

Odd Jobs

- Mow weekly and leave clippings on the lawn.
- Turn compost pile as needed.
- Mulch all bare soil. Don't pile mulch on trunks and stems of plants.
- Feed and water the birds!

JULY

Plant

- Color for fall, including aster, celosia, cosmos, marigold, morning glory, Joseph's coat, ornamental grasses, Mexican bush sage, and zinnia.
- Container-grown nursery stock and field-grown trees.
- Warm-season lawn grasses.
- Herbs such as basil, lemongrass, lemon verbena, oregano, thyme, etc.
- Melons, peppers, tomatoes, and other warm-season vegetables for fall garden. Plant pumpkin seeds around

July 4 for jack-o'-lanterns for Halloween. Also plant beans, black-eyed peas, cantaloupe, chard, cucumber, eggplant, New Zealand and Malabar spinach, and summer and winter squash.
- Wildflower seed—better to plant now than to wait until fall.

Fertilize

- All planting areas with organic fertilizers, if not done in June.
- Use Texas greensand for iron and trace mineral deficiency.
- Use high-calcium lime for calcium deficiency. Also drench with fireplace ashes and water. Use 1 rounded tablespoon per gallon of water.
- Foliar-feed with Garrett Juice or aerated compost tea on all foliage. Drench the soil around plants as well.
- Avoid synthetic high-nitrogen salt-based fertilizers, especially nitrogen-only choices.

Prune

- Trees and shrubs if needed—no flush cuts.
- Roses lightly to encourage fall bloom.
- Flower heads off crape myrtles to encourage rebloom.

Water

- Carefully and efficiently during drought periods.
- All planting areas deeply but infrequently during dry periods.
- Outdoor container plants daily, others as needed.

Pest Control

- Sooty mold and powdery mildew on crape myrtles: Spray Plant Wash or cornmeal tea.
- Cinch bugs: Dust natural diatomaceous earth in dry weather or spray the orange-oil-based fire ant control mound-drench formula.
- Elm leaf beetles, lacebugs: Spray summer-weight horticultural oil or orange-oil-based mound-drench products. Use *Bacillus thuringiensis* (Bt) on caterpillar-infested plants only.
- Spider mites: Spray garlic-pepper tea or any spray that contains liquid seaweed.
- Fire ants: Drench with one of the mound-drench products. Apply Spinosad product. Apply beneficial nematodes. Dust mounds with cinnamon.
- Fleas, ticks, chiggers, Bermuda mites: Dust natural diatomaceous earth during dry weather. Spray orange-

oil mound-drench products and apply beneficial nematodes anytime, but especially during wet weather. Dust with very light amounts of sulfur in alkaline soils.

- Webworms, bagworms, leaf rollers, and other worms of moths and butterflies: Spray *Bacillus thuringiensis* (Bt) with 1 ounce of molasses per gallon of water. Spray at dusk. Release trichogramma wasps next year when leaves first emerge in the spring.
- Scale insects on euonymus, hollies, and camellias: Spray horticultural oil or fire ant mound-drench formula or remove the unadapted plants.
- Weeds: Hand remove or use mechanical devices. Spray vinegar-based herbicides if needed.
- Mosquitoes: Spray garlic tea or one of the plant oil products and apply dry garlic to the soil and pots.

Odd Jobs

- Build beds for the fall vegetable garden or ornamental plants. Prepare new beds with quality compost, expanded shale, lava sand, greensand, dry molasses, and horticultural or whole ground cornmeal. Work amendments into the native soil. If possible, prepare beds under trees with an air spade to prevent injury to roots.
- Mow weekly or as needed and leave clippings on the lawn.
- Turn compost pile, add new ingredients, and start new piles. Add molasses to piles to stimulate biological activity and eliminate problems with fire ants.
- Mulch all bare soil with partially completed compost or other coarse-textured natural material. Shredded native tree mulch is the best choice.
- Feed and water the birds!

AUGUST

Plant

- Copper canyon daisy, marigold, portulaca, purslane, zinnia, wildflowers, and ornamental grasses for immediate color. Many great types of salvia are available.
- Finish planting warm-season lawn grasses—Bermuda, St. Augustine, zoysia.
- Horseherb and other ground covers in shady areas where turf is struggling.
- Wildflower seed if you haven't already.
- Too early to plant pansies.

Fertilize

- Foliar-feed all plantings with Garrett Juice. Also

drench the soil of any new or struggling plants.
- If you haven't done so yet this year, apply dry molasses at a rate of 10 lbs. per 1,000 sq. ft. Do not fertilize wildflower areas.

Prune

- Declining flowering plants to encourage more blooms.
- Dead and damaged wood from shrubs and trees. No flush cuts or pruning dressings or paints.

Water

- As deeply and as infrequently as possible. Your garden and landscape will usually need more water this month than any other.
- Potted plants and hanging baskets need water daily. Expanded shale and/or lava sand added to the soil as mulch will greatly help hold moisture and reduce watering needs.
- Be especially careful of azalea beds and other sensitive plants.

Pest Control

- Spray Plant Wash for general insect pest and disease control if needed.
- Grubworms: Good soil culture is the best control. Apply molasses and beneficial nematodes as needed.
- Chinch bugs: Dust natural diatomaceous earth or spray one of the orange-oil-based pest control products or another of the plant-oil products. Do not use pyrethrum products for this or any other pest.
- Aphids: Apply Garrett Juice and garlic tea. Use water blasts and release ladybugs. Add 2 oz. molasses per gallon of spray.
- Fire ants: Dust natural diatomaceous earth or spray one of the orange-oil-based pest control products or any of the other plant-oil products. Apply beneficial nematodes. Broadcast orange or grapefruit peelings and pulp. Horticultural cornmeal also helps. The application of grits continues to provide strong reports of effectiveness.
- Chewing insects: Dust natural diatomaceous earth or spray Garret Juice plus garlic-pepper tea. Spray plant-oil products such as Bioganic or Eco-EXEMPT if needed. Add 2 oz. of orange oil or d-limonene per gallon for the hard-to-control insects. Broadcast beneficial nematodes.
- Cabbage loopers and other caterpillars: Release trichogramma wasps and spray *Bacillus thuringiensis* (Bt)

products at dusk with molasses added at 2 oz. per gallon of spray.

- Mosquitoes: Spray or mist one of the plant-oil products (not pyrethrum) and apply dry granulated garlic at 10–20 lbs. per 1,000 sq. ft.
- Borers in peaches, plums, and other fruit trees: Use the Organic Fruit and Pecan Tree Program (download from www.dirtdoctor.com). Apply d-limonene or orange oil to the affected parts of the trunks. Mix into a 50/50 solution with water.
- Brown patch in turf: Treat with whole ground cornmeal or dry granulated garlic. Spray plant wash.

Odd Jobs

- Mow weekly and leave clippings on the lawn.
- Turn compost pile.
- Spray weeds in walks, driveways, and terraces with vinegar. Use 10% or 100 grain vinegar with 1 oz. of orange oil and 1 tsp. of liquid soap and 1 tbsp. of molasses per gallon. Carefully spot-spray in beds and turf. Do not use toxic chemical products.
- Don't forget to feed and water the birds!

SEPTEMBER

Plant

- Wildflower seeds if you didn't plant them at the best time in summer.
- Fall-blooming perennials, such as asters and mums, and hardy perennials, especially spring-blooming plants. Divide spring-blooming perennials if necessary.
- Cool-season vegetables, including beets, broccoli, Brussels sprouts, cabbage, carrots, cauliflower, English peas, lettuce, potatoes, radishes, spinach, and turnips.
- Fall vegetable garden plants, especially the warm-weather veggies like tomatoes.
- Finish warm-season lawn grass plantings of Bermuda and zoysia by seed no later than early September. Solid sod can be planted year-round.
- Transplant established spring-flowering bulbs, daylilies, daisies, iris, and peonies.

Fertilize

- All planting areas with an organic fertilizer at approximately 10–20 lbs. per 1,000 sq. ft. in the **third major fertilization of the year**. Corn gluten meal can be used to help control annual winter weeds such as (*Poa*

annua) bluegrass, dandelion, fescuegrass, ryegrass.
- Foliar-feed all planting areas and lawns with Garrett Juice. Drench the soil of new and problems plants.
- Avoid all synthetic fertilizers but especially the weed-and-feed and nitrogen-only types. Remember that the only complete, balanced fertilizers are organic.

Prune

- Roots of wisterias that failed to bloom in the past.
- Remove spent blooms of summer-flowering perennials if you haven't already.
- Remove surface tree roots if you have to, but no more than 20% of root system per year. It's best to leave the roots and add shredded tree-trimming mulch.

Water

- Water deeply but only as needed during dry spells.
- Potted plants and hanging baskets regularly. Add Garrett Juice as a root stimulator for better performance.

Pest Control

- Brown patch or take-all patch in St. Augustine: Apply horticultural cornmeal at 10–20 lbs. per 1,000 sq. ft. For follow-up applications, use dry or liquid garlic, potassium bicarbonate, or cornmeal juice. Dry granulated garlic at 2 lbs. per 1,000 sq. ft. also works well.
- Webworms, tent caterpillars: Use *Bacillus thuringiensis* (Bt) as a last resort on infected plants only. Spinosad is also effective. Make a note to release trichogramma wasps next spring.
- Grubworms: Apply beneficial nematodes if necessary, but realize that only 10% of the grubs you see are harmful to plants.
- Cabbage loopers on broccoli, Brussels sprouts, cabbage, cauliflower: Spray *Bacillus thuringiensis* (Bt). Release trichogramma wasps prior to this time next year.
- Aphids on tender new fall growth: Spray garlic tea or water blasts and release ladybugs. Add 1–2 ounces of molasses per gallon of spray. Spinosad can also be used.
- Fire ants: Drench mounds with orange-oil-based mound-drench or plant-oil product and apply beneficial nematodes. Apply Spinosad product for problem infestations.
- Black spot and powdery mildew on roses: Spray garlic-pepper tea and see the Organic Rose Program on the Web site, www.dirtdoctor.com.
- Weeds: Chemicals pushers recommend MSMA. It's an idiotic recommendation. The product contains an

arsenic compound. They also recommend 2,4-D products for broadleaf weeds and products like Manage for other weeds. These chemicals will severely injure or kill your trees. Image is a waste of money and can do damage to desirable plants.

- Iron chlorosis (yellow leaves, dark green veins, newest growth first): Apply the entire Sick Tree Treatment and add Epsom salts or Sul-Po-Mag if magnesium is deficient in the soil. Texas greensand can help because it contains many trace minerals. Iron may not be the only deficiency. The key is to stimulate the biological activity of the soil so that the "tied-up" minerals in the soil are made available to plants.

Odd Jobs

- Mow weekly and leave clippings on the lawn.
- Turn the compost pile.
- Feed and water the birds!

OCTOBER

Plant

- Cool-season leaf and root crops such as beets, Brussels sprouts, cabbage, carrots, collard greens, garlic, lettuce, onions, spinach, strawberries, and turnips.
- Cyclamen, dianthus, English daisies, flowering cabbage and kale, poppies, nasturtium, pansies, pinks, snapdragons, violas, wallflowers, and other cool-season flowers.
- All the perennial herbs as well as coriander, dill, and parsley.
- Hardy perennials, especially spring-flowering plants.
- Wildflower seeds if you haven't planted them already.
- Trees, shrubs, vines, and spring- and summer-flowering perennials.
- Cool-season grasses such as rye and fescue. It is also time to plant clover, vetch, Austrian winter peas, and other cool-season crops.
- Finish warm-season lawn grass plantings by seed by early October. Quality solid sod can be planted anytime that quality grass is available.
- Transplant established spring-flowering bulbs, daisies, daylilies, iris, peonies, etc., if necessary.

Fertilize

- Broadcast dry molasses for any plants not looking well. Feed all planting areas with an organic fertilizer at approximately 10–20 lbs. per 1,000 sq. ft.

- Foliar-feed all planting areas and lawns with compost tea or Garrett Juice. Make sure to include seaweed in whatever mix you use. Drench potted plants with the same mixture. Fish emulsion should be added for more punch.

Prune

- Tree limbs that are broken, diseased, or in the way; dangerous limbs that might fall ASAP. Do not make flush cuts, use no pruning paint or wound dressing, and do not overprune any trees.
- Oleanders if needed.
- Root-prune wisterias that have failed to bloom. This may or may not help.
- Remove spent blooms of summer-flowering perennials.
- Do not prune knees from bald cypress trees—they are part of the root system. Instead, change the root-zone areas from grass to ground cover or mulch.

Water

- All plants deeply during dry spells.
- Potted plants and hanging baskets regularly as needed. Add compost tea or Garrett Juice for weak plants.

Pest Control

- Brown patch in St. Augustine: Spray Garrett Juice plus garlic tea or cornmeal juice. Apply horticultural cornmeal at 10–20 lbs. per 1,000 sq. ft. or dry granulated garlic at 2 lbs. per 1,000 sq. ft.
- Webworms, tent caterpillars, cabbage loopers, and other caterpillars: Spray Spinosad or *Bacillus thuringiensis* (Bt) as a last resort on infested plants only. Add 1–2 oz. of molasses per gallon of water and spray at dusk. Release trichogramma wasps next spring for prevention.
- Grubworms: Apply beneficial nematodes if necessary. Most grubworms are beneficial.
- Aphids on tender new fall growth: Use a strong garlic-pepper tea or water blast followed by release of ladybugs. Add 1–2 oz. of molasses per gallon of spray. Use plant-oil sprays for serious problems. Correct the plant stress, or they will be back.
- Fire ants: Drench mounds with orange-oil-based products or plant-oil products and later release beneficial nematodes. Some gardeners continue to have success with regular grits, cornmeal, and dry molasses.
- Black spot, powdery mildew, and other fungal diseases: Apply the Sick Tree Treatment and spray

plants with garlic tea, garlic-pepper tea, or plant wash.

■ Chlorosis (yellow leaves, dark green veins on new growth first): Apply the entire Sick Tree Treatment and add a trace mineral product to the Garrett Juice. Apply Texas greensand at 40 lbs. per 1,000 sq. ft. Greensand is important because it contains many trace minerals. Iron may not be (probably isn't) the only deficiency.

■ Spray weeds and grass around tree trunks with vinegar. Use full strength 9%–10% vinegar with 1 oz. orange oil, 1 tsp. liquid soap, and 1 tbsp. molasses per gallon.

Odd Jobs

■ Mulch all bare soil with shredded tree trimmings. Shredded material from your own property is best; composted mulch is the best to purchase. Rubber, colored wood, and pine bark should be avoided.

■ Mow weekly and leave the clippings on the lawn. Those with buffalograss can mow less often, as little as once a year.

■ Build new compost piles, turn old ones, and water dry ones.

■ Use quality compost and other organic amendments to prepare new planting beds. To reflower a poinsettia, give it uninterrupted darkness 14 hours each day and 10 hours of bright light each day until December. It's better to buy new plants each year.

■ Use compost or shredded tree trimmings as a top-dressing mulch for ornamentals and vegetables.

■ Feed and water the birds!

NOVEMBER

Plant

■ Trees, shrubs, vines, ground covers, and tough perennials.

■ Spring bulbs, including daffodils and grape hyacinths. Pre-cool tulips and Dutch hyacinths for 45 days at 40° prior to planting. Don't plant them now.

■ Cyclamen, dianthus, English daisies, flowering cabbage and kale, garlic, Iceland poppies, nasturtium, pansies, pinks, snapdragons, violas, wallflowers, and other cool-season flowers.

■ Transplant spring- and summer-flowering perennials, including daisies, daylilies, iris, lilies, thrift, etc.

■ Bluebonnets, coreopsis, cosmos, gaillardia, Indian paintbrush, larkspur, phlox, and poppies from seed.

■ Finish planting cool-season spring-flowering annuals, including English daisies, flowering cabbage and kale,

pansies, pinks, snapdragons, and California and Iceland poppies.

■ Cool-season grasses.

Fertilize

■ Bulbs, annuals, and perennials with earthworm castings and other gentle, organic fertilizers.

■ Indoor plants with earthworm castings, lava sand, coffee grounds, and other low-odor organic fertilizers.

■ Cool-season grasses with organic fertilizer at ½ rates.

■ Apply ½" of compost to poorly performing turf areas.

Prune

■ Remove all vines from trees.

■ Remove ground covers, grasses, and soils from the bases of trees.

■ Begin major tree pruning if needed. Protect the branch collars by never making flush cuts. Remove dead limbs if possible before leaves fall.

■ Pick-prune shrubs to remove longest shoots if needed.

■ Remove spent blooms on annuals and perennials or leave the seed heads on flowering plants for the birds.

■ Cut off tops of brown perennials. Remove spent annuals, but leave roots in the soil.

Water

■ All planting areas at least once if no rain. Add 1 tablespoon of apple cider vinegar to each gallon of water used on indoor and outdoor potted plants.

Pest Control

■ Check the roots of removed annuals and other suspicious plants for nematodes (knots on the roots). Treat infected soil with biostimulants, molasses, compost, and citrus pulp.

■ Check houseplants for spider mites, scale, and aphids. Apply horticultural cornmeal to the soil. Spray as needed with biostimulants and mild soap and seaweed products. Use plant oils and lightweight horticultural oils as a last resort.

■ Watch lawn for signs of grubworm damage. Grass will be loose and not connected to the soil. Treat with dry molasses or beneficial nematodes. These insects are rarely a problem for organic gardeners with healthy soil.

■ If brown patch is still showing in turf, treat with horticultural or whole ground cornmeal and drench with garlic tea if the problem persists.

Odd Jobs

- If you want to know the baseline chemistry of your soil, send soil samples to Texas Plant & Soil Lab in Edinburgh, Texas. See link on dirtdoctor.com for details.
- Pick tomatoes the day before the first freeze. Let them ripen indoors.
- Put spent annuals and other vegetative matter into the compost piles. Mulch the fallen leaves into the turf. Put excesses in beds or in the compost pile.
- Add mulch to cover all bare soil. Do not till or plow once healthy soil has been developed in the vegetable garden.
- Mulch all bare ornamental beds for winter protection.
- Turn compost piles as time allows.
- Feed and water the birds!

DECEMBER

Plant

- Cool-season annuals and hardy perennials; delphiniums, larkspur, and poppies from seed. Many cool-season transplant choices are available.
- Trees, shrubs, vines, ground covers, and other crops such as arugula, cabbage, chard, greens, kale, lettuce, and spinach. Carrots and garlic can still be planted.
- Herb transplants, including coriander, dill, fennel lavender, oregano, parsley, rosemary, rue, and sage. Dill and fennel may need some freeze protection.
- Living Christmas trees (after use) that are adapted to the area's climate and soils.
- Spring bulbs, including tulips and hyacinths.
- Transplant shrubs and trees.

Fertilize

- Avoid all synthetic fertilizers, of course.
- Cool-season annuals in beds and pots. Use Garrett Juice as a soil-drench fertilizer. Include products with mycorrhizal fungi.
- Greenhouse plants if needed with organic fertilizers, earthworm castings, and lava sand.
- Houseplants once during the winter with earthworm castings, lava sand, and other odorless organic fertilizers. Coffee grounds are one good choice. Add apple cider vinegar at 1 tbsp. to 1 oz. per gallon at each watering.
- Winter grasses with mild organic fertilizer at ½ rate, usually 10 lbs. per 1,000 sq. ft.

Prune

- Do not prune the tops of crape myrtles. The seed pods are decorative, and some birds like the seed.
- Evergreens to adjust the appearance.
- Shade trees to remove dead, damaged, and out-of-place limbs. Do not prune just to "thin out" trees. Trimming can be done to avoid crowding and to allow more light to understory plants.
- Do not make flush cuts and do not apply pruning paint to any plants.
- Cut off tops of spent perennials if not already done, but leave roots in the ground.
- Wait till the end of the winter to prune fruit trees and grapes. Best timing for them is just before bud break to prevent premature flowering.
- Use the dormant months to remove ground covers from the bases of plants and vines completely from all trees. If soil is on the root flares and trunks of trees, remove the soil very carefully with slow water and a Shop Vac. A stiff broom works well on slightly moist soil. It's best to hire an arborist to do the work with the air spade.

Water

- Potted plants as needed.
- Any dry areas to help protect against desiccation and winter cold injury.
- Add apple cider vinegar at 1 tbsp. to 1 oz. per gallon, time permitting.

Pest Control

- Bark aphids on trees look scary, but normally need no treatment.
- Spray heavy infestations of scale insects on shade and fruit trees with horticultural oil—not recommended except in extreme cases, as sprays will kill beneficial insects and microbes.
- Cut mistletoe out of trees, remove infested limbs if possible, and apply the Sick Tree Treatment. Also apply the Sick Tree Treatment to other stressed trees, such as those with heavy infestations of galls.
- Spray houseplants with liquid seaweed, mild soap, and biostimulants to control scale, mealybugs, spider mites, and other insects. Mild mound-drench solutions can also be used.
- Avoid all toxic chemical pesticides, as usual.
- Spray garlic tea on plants with fungal diseases. Apply

dry granulated garlic to the soil for additional control.

■ Remember that henbit, clover, and other wildflowers are beautiful, so don't worry about spraying them in most cases. If you must, spray the vinegar herbicides between Christmas and New Year's Day. The formula is 1 gal. 10% vinegar, 1 oz. orange oil, 1 tbsp. molasses, and 1 tsp. Plant Wash.

Odd Jobs

■ Continue to mulch leaves into the turf.

■ Cover tender plants before freezes with floating row cover. Potted plants can be covered with large trash cans.

■ Pick tomatoes the night before first freeze, unless they are already gone.

■ Clean and oil tools before storing for winter.

■ Run mower and trimmer engines dry of gasoline. Drain and change oil. Take to repair shop now to avoid the spring rush.

■ Mulch all bare soil. Apply a thin layer of compost followed by shredded native tree trimmings.

■ Turn compost piles as time allows. Add molasses to speed up breakdown.

■ Apply lava or decomposed granite on icy paving. Do not use chemical de-icers, salt, and synthetic fertilizers.

■ Feed and water the birds!

Acacia

Anacua

Anacua

ACACIA: Over 1,200 species, 20 or so in cultivation. Many are fragrant in bloom. As a group, they are fast-growing and short-lived (20–30 years). Should not be fertilized, as fertilization and irrigation will shorten their life. Generally propagated by seed. Many do well in Houston.

ANACUA
Sandpaper Tree, Knockaway
Ehretia anacua
(eh-REE-shah ah-NOK-you-ah or ah-NOK-wha)

Evergreen—Sun
Ht. 30'–50' Spread 30'
Spacing 30'–40'

HABIT: Grows in alkaline soils with good drainage, but can also survive in slightly acid sands. Crown is very dense and creates heavy shade. Mature trees have a distinctive gnarled appearance and are often multitrunked. Blooms from late fall through winter into the early spring, depending on rain and climate. May have more than one blooming period. Flowers are pure white and fragrant. Spring-ripening fruits are bright orange drupes about the size of hackberries. Foliage is dark green, almost evergreen, and has a rough sandpaper texture.

CULTURE: Anacua needs plenty of water to establish and then becomes very drought tolerant. After establishment, it can be killed by overwatering or poor drainage. Very little if any fertilizer is needed.

USES: Shade tree.

PROBLEMS: Few other than poor drainage, improper planting, or environmental damage.

NOTES: Anacua is native to southern Texas. Great honeybee attractant and food source for wildlife.

ASH, GREEN
River Ash
Fraxinus pennsylvanica
(FRAK-suh-nus pen-cil-VAN-ika)

Fast-growing deciduous tree with large compound leaves, dark green foliage, yellow fall color. Smooth, mottled bark when young that gets rougher with age. Easy to grow to 40' in any soil. Medium water, light fertilization. Shade tree, fall color, background tree, mass tree planting. Not extremely high quality.

Green Ash

ASH, PRICKLY
Toothache Tree
Zanthoxylum clava-herculis
(zanth-OX-ih-lum CLA-va her-CUE-lis)

Small deciduous tree to 30'. Normally found along hedgerows, in thickets, and on edges of forests in East Texas but also spreading farther west. Adapted to a wide range of soils and prefers full sun. It likes deep, heavily alkaline clay soils but will also grow in almost sterile sands. Easy to grow in most any soil. Not really recommended for planting, but it is easy to keep alive if it already exists on site. Seldom planted.

ASH, TEXAS
White Ash
Fraxinus texensis
(FRAK-suh-nus tex-EN-sis)

Deciduous—Sun
Ht. 50' Spread 40'
Spacing 20'–30'

HABIT: Medium growth, large compound leaves with rounded leaflets, especially on young growth. White splotches on trunk and limbs. Orange to purple fall color.

CULTURE: Easy to grow in any soil. Grows readily in alkaline soil, rock, or steep slopes. Low water and fertilization needs. Needs excellent drainage. Easy to transplant.
USES: Shade tree, fall color.
PROBLEMS: Poor drainage, borers.
NOTES: One of Texas's best-kept secrets. Close kin or the same as white ash (*F. americana*)—also a good tree. Should be used much more. Native to Texas. Several white ash cultivars are available.

Texas Ash

41

BIRCH, RIVER
Water Birch
Betula nigra
(BET-ew-la NYE-gruh)

Deciduous—Sun
Ht. 30'–50' Spread 15'–20'
Spacing 20'–25'

HABIT: The trunk generally divides low into several upright trunks. Young bark is smooth and pinkish; bark on older trees is brown, flaky, and curling. Diamond-shaped leaves. Yellow fall color.
CULTURE: Needs plenty of moisture and does well in wet soils. Very fast-growing but not long-lived.
USES: Shade tree or specimen tree.
PROBLEMS: Does not do well in heavy alkaline clay soils without enough moisture.
NOTES: Interesting tree but not highly recommended in Texas. Does well in an organic program.

River Birch

BIRD OF PARADISE
Caesalpinia gilliesii
(kie-sal-PEEN-ee-uh gil-EEZ-ee-eye)

Deciduous—Sun
Ht. 8'–15' Spread 10'–15'
Spacing 8'–10'

HABIT: Small decorative tree or large shrub, dramatic yellow flowers with red stamens spring and summer. Finely textured interesting foliage. Is kin to the pride of Barbados, which is used more as a perennial.
CULTURE: Easy to grow, any soil, drought tolerant.
USES: Ornamental tree, yellow summer flowers.
PROBLEMS: Few if any.
NOTES: Native from central United States to Texas, Argentina, and Uruguay. *C. mexicana* is a yellow-flowering Texas native that grows wild in the far southern tip of the state.

Bird of Paradise

BLACK GUM
Nyssa sylvatica var. *sylvatica*
(NI-sa sil-VA-ti-ka)

Deciduous—Sun
Ht. 50'–100' Spread 30'
Spacing 30'

HABIT: Clusters of shiny blue-black fruit enjoyed by many wild animals. Foliage is shiny green in the summer and scarlet in the fall. A few leaves will sometimes turn red in the late summer. One of the best Texas trees for fall color. Relatively slow-growing.
CULTURE: Unfortunately, it won't grow in alkaline soils. Prefers East Texas acid sand or Houston-area clays. Likes moist to wet soils best.
USES: Shade tree, fall color.
PROBLEMS: Needs acid soil.
NOTES: *Nyssa* also includes the East Texas tupelo tree. *N. aquatica* is water

tupelo. *N. sylvatica* var. *biflora* is the swamp tupelo. All these trees can grow well over 100' tall in the right conditions.

Black Gum

BUCKEYE, MEXICAN

Ungnadia speciosa
(oong-NAY-dee-uh spee-see-OH-suh)

Deciduous—Sun/Part Shade
Ht. 20' Spread 40'
Spacing 10'–20'

HABIT: Moderate growth, fragrant purple flowers in spring. Brilliant yellow fall color. Decorative three-pod seeds on bare branches in winter.

Mexican Buckeye

CULTURE: Easy, any soil, little fertilization. Although drought tolerant, can stand irrigation if drainage is good.
USES: Spring and fall color, understory tree, specimen courtyard tree.
PROBLEMS: Few if any.
NOTES: Can be easily grown from seed. The sweet seeds are poisonous to humans. Great tree—should be used more. Native to Texas and Mexico.

BUCKEYE, TEXAS

(*Aesculus glabra*) Small native tree to 30', white flowers in spring. Foliage looks similar to chestnut. Grows well in alkaline soils, sun, or partial shade. *A. glabra* var. *glabra,* the Ohio buckeye, is not as well adapted in Texas. *A. pavia* var. *pavia*, the red buckeye or scarlet buckeye, reaches heights of 15'–25' and has red flower spikes in spring. Most buckeyes turn yellow, then lose their foliage in the heat of summer. Don't worry—that's normal.

Camphor Tree

CAMPHOR TREE

Cinnamomum camphora
(sin-ah-MO-mum cam-FOE-rah)

Evergreen—Full Sun
Ht. 40'–50' Spread 30'
Spacing 20'–30'

HABIT: Clusters of very small, fragrant white flowers in late spring, followed by small black fruits. Beautiful shiny fragrant leaves that smell like camphor.
CULTURE: Needs protection in severe winters, and excellent drainage is critical.
USES: Potpourri, specimen tree.
PROBLEMS: Roots are very competitive. May freeze at 20° and below. Possible root rot. Considered to be an invasive plant.
NOTES: The official tree of Hiroshima because it survived the atomic bombing.

Carolina Basswood

CAROLINA BASSWOOD

(*Tilia caroliniana*) Texas native linden that grows wild in East and South Central Texas. It grows up to 90' in deep, rich soils and has fragrant flowers from April to June. Kin to little leaf linden.

CATALPA

Indian Bean, Fish Bait Tree, Cigar Tree
(*Catalpa bignonioides*) Large, fast-growing, open-branching shade tree with smoothish bark, very large light green leaves, dramatic white flower clusters in early summer, and cigarlike seedpods in the fall. Very easy to grow in any soil; rarely needs pruning. Grown in East Texas to attract black caterpillars for fishing. Shade tree for large estates, parks, golf courses. Some say the flowers and leaves are messy, but I like this tree. Native to the southern United States and has naturalized in Texas.

CEDAR, EASTERN RED

Juniperus virginiana
(joo-NIP-ur-us ver-jin-ee-AN-uh)

Evergreen—Sun
Ht. 40' Spread 20'
Spacing 20'–30'

HABIT: Single trunk, upright and conical when young, spreading with age. Dark green juniper-like foliage; hard, fragrant wood. Females have blue berries in fall and winter.
CULTURE: Very easy to grow in any soil (even solid rock). Drought tolerant.
USES: Shade tree, screen for bad views, evergreen backdrop.
PROBLEMS: Bagworms, red spider mites on stressed trees.
NOTES: Is becoming more available as a nursery-grown tree. Many are allergic to the pollen, but it's in the air already from the wild trees. Native to eastern United States and Texas. Mountain cedar (*J. ashei*) is similar but usually has multiple-stem trunk, flakier bark, and does not suffer cedar apple rust fungus.

Eastern Red Cedar

CEDAR, INCENSE

(*Calocedrus decurrens*) Tall and straight, single dominant trunk; bark looks like redwood tree, foliage like arborvitae. Great-looking tree but is hard to find in nurseries.

Incense Cedar

CHERRY, BLACK
Wild Cherry, Choke Cherry
Prunus serotina
(PROO-nus ser-oh-TEE-nah)

Deciduous—Sun
Ht. 25'–50' Spread 25'–30'
Spacing 25'–30'

HABIT: White drooping flowers when leaves have just emerged, followed by clusters of green, red, and black cherries, which can all be on the tree at the same time. Most of the fruit ripens in late summer. Beautiful shiny foliage. Yellow fall color.
CULTURE: Needs moist, well-drained soil.
USES: Ornamental tree, high-quality wood. Food for birds and other wildlife.
PROBLEMS: Tent caterpillars. Twigs and leaves can be toxic to animals and humans.
NOTES: Can grow to over 100' in the deep sandy soils. The escarpment black cherry is *Prunus serotina eximia*. Black cherry makes a fine landscape tree and should be used more. Herbalists recommend cherries and cherry juice for intestinal cleaning. Black cherry is an important food source for wildlife.

Black Cherry

CHERRY LAUREL
Carolina Cherry
Prunus caroliniana
(PROO-nus ka-ro-lin-ee-AN-uh)

Evergreen—Sun/Shade
Ht. 25' Spread 15'
Spacing 8'–15'

HABIT: Upright bushy growth, can be trimmed into tree form. White flowers along stems in spring. 'Bright and Tight' and 'Compacta' are improved compact cultivars.
CULTURE: Will grow in any soil, but is not long-lived.
USES: Evergreen screen, small ornamental.
PROBLEMS: Borers, cotton root rot, crown gall, chlorosis, and ice-storm damage.
NOTES: There are much better choices. Native from eastern United States to Texas. Leaves and branches are poisonous.

Cherry Laurel

CHITTAMWOOD

(*Bumelia lanuginosa*) Deciduous slow-growing, upright tree with dark stiff branches, thorns, and small leaves similar to live oak. Yellow fall color. Resembles live oak at a distance. Borers can be a problem.

CITRUS

Citrus grows fairly well here. Remember that cold hardiness is increased several degrees for plants grown organically, and flavor is also increased. Citrus are heavy users of magnesium. Use Epsom salts or Sul-Po-Mag yearly. Many varieties do well in Houston, including lemons, limes, tangerines, oranges, grapefruits, and kumquats. *C. meyeri*—Meyer lemon—is not a true lemon but is thought to be a cross between a lemon and a sweet orange. *C. reticulata*—Satsuma orange or Satsuma mandarin—is of high quality and the most cold-tolerant citrus for Houston.

CLETHRA

Mexican Clethra, Mexican Sweetspire (*Clethra pringlei*)
Small upright evergreen tree with dark green glossy foliage, racemes of fragrant creamy white flowers in summer. Plant in full sun to light shade and enjoy the cinnamon aroma in the garden. Grows to 20' height.

CRABAPPLE

(*Malus* spp.) Deciduous ornamental tree to 25'. Spring flowers (white, red, pink); half-inch fruit matures in fall. Sun or part shade. At least 500 species exist. *M. floribunda* has white flowers with a pink tinge. 'Snowdrift' has white flowers, orange-red fruit. 'Sargent' has white flowers, dark red fruit. 'Callaway' has light pink flowers, large red fruit. 'Radiant' has single red flowers, red fruit. Native to China and Japan.

CRAPE MYRTLE

Lagerstroemia indica
(lah-ger-STROH-me-uh IN-dih-kuh)

Deciduous—Sun
Ht. 25' Spread 15'
Spacing 15'–20'

HABIT: Slow-growing, light smooth bark, small oval leaves, flowers all summer (red, purple, pink, white). Fall color ranges from yellow to purple.
CULTURE: Very easy to grow in any soil. Add rock phosphate to regular program to help

Chittamwood

Clethra

Crape Myrtle

46

flower production. Do not trim back in winter—it does not increase flower production; besides, the seedpods are decorative and finches like them.

USES: Ornamental tree, summer color, fall color, beautiful bare branches in winter.

PROBLEMS: Aphids, mildew, suckers at the ground.

NOTES: 'Glendora White' is one of my favorites. There are many great choices, including 'Dynamite', 'Royal Velvet', and 'Natchez', with the beautiful exfoliating bark. Native to China.

Crape Myrtle

CYPRESS, BALD

Taxodium distichum
(tax-OH-dee-um DIS-tick-um)

Deciduous—Sun
Ht. 80' Spread 50'
Spacing 20'–40'

HABIT: Moderately fast-growing, upright, pyramidal when young but spreading with age. Light green lacy foliage, reddish brown fall color. Branching structure is layered and distinctive. Root "knees" will appear, especially in moist or wet soil.

CULTURE: Easy to grow in any soil except solid rock. Drought tolerant, although can grow in wet areas. Cannot take any shade—must have full sun to avoid limb dieback. Can become chlorotic in alkaline soils.

USES: Specimen, shade tree, background tree, fall color, delicate foliage texture.

PROBLEMS: Chlorosis and crown gall occasionally, bagworms.

NOTES: Likes well-drained soils best. The often-seen lake habitation results from a seed germination need and a protection against prairie fires through the years. Native from eastern United States to Texas.

Bald Cypress

Montezuma Cypress

CYPRESS, MONTEZUMA

Water Larch
Taxodium mucronatum
(tax-OH-dee-um mew-crow-NAY-tum)

Semi-evergreen—Sun
Ht. 80' Spread 50'
Spacing 30'–50'

HABIT: Large-growing graceful tree that is similar to bald cypress but better in many ways. It is almost totally evergreen, grows much faster, doesn't get brown in late winter, and doesn't have the knees from the root system.

CULTURE: Same requirements as bald cypress but is even easier to grow. Will grow in wet soils or in normally moist soils. As with all cypress trees, full sun is an absolute requirement. Responds to fertilizer but is not a heavy feeder.

USES: Shade or specimen tree.

PROBLEMS: Freeze damage is not nearly the problem that has been reported.

Montezuma Cypress

Pond Cypress

NOTES: One of the very best trees that can be planted along the Gulf Coast. As a side note, it grows very well in most of the state. The largest one in the world is the Tule Tree just south of Oaxaca, Mexico.

CYPRESS, POND
Taxodium ascendens
(tax-OH-dee-um uh-SEND-enz)

Deciduous—Sun
Ht. 70' Spread 30'
Spacing 20'–40'

HABIT: Rapid growth, narrower than regular bald cypress, green earlier in spring and longer into fall. Leaflets spiral out from the stem and do not open. Long, delicate filament-like leaves. Lovely, soft overall appearance. Rust fall color.

CULTURE: Easy to grow in most soils with normal water and nutrient requirements. Can tolerate wet soil.

USES: Specimen, shade tree, mass planting, background tree.

PROBLEMS: Availability.

NOTES: Is not becoming more available. Also called *T. distichum* 'Nutans'.

DOGWOOD, FLOWERING
Cornus florida
(KOR-nus FLOR-ih-duh)

Deciduous—Shade/Part Shade
Ht. 20' Spread 20'
Spacing 15'–20'

HABIT: Graceful, layered structure. Pink or white flowers in spring. Red fall color.

CULTURE: Needs loose, acid, well-drained soil. Needs plenty of moisture, but drainage is a must. Will do best in beds with heavy percentage of organic material.

USES: Ornamental tree, spring flowers, red fall color. Excellent choice for Houston gardeners.

PROBLEMS: Cotton root rot, borers in unhealthy plants. Will normally be chlorotic in high-pH soils.

NOTES: Would not be considered a low-maintenance plant. This tree is native to acid, sandy soils like those in East Texas. Many improved cultivars available.

Flowering Dogwood

DOGWOOD, ROUGH-LEAF
Cornus drummondii
(KOR-nus druh-MUN-dee-eye)

Deciduous—Sun/Shade
Ht. 15' Spread 15'
Spacing 6'–12'

HABIT: Shrubby, small tree, blooms with white flower clusters after leaves have formed in late spring. White seedpods in late summer and purple fall color. Plant spreads easily by seeds and suckers but is not a problem. Stems are reddish and very decorative in winter.
CULTURE: Very easy to grow in any soil, drought tolerant.
USES: Background mass, understory tree, seeds for birds.
PROBLEMS: Few, if any, other than cosmetic leaf spotting diseases.
NOTES: Many have been cut down by people thinking they are weeds. This plant is graceful, tough, and should be used more. Native from eastern United States to Texas.

Rough-leaf Dogwood

ELM, AMERICAN
Ulmus americana
(ULL-mus uh-mair-ih-KAY-nuh)

Deciduous—Sun
Ht. 70' Spread 70'
Spacing 40'–50'

HABIT: Fast-growing, gracefully spreading, large leaves, yellow fall color.
CULTURE: Easy to grow in any soil with normal water and nutrients.
USES: Shade tree, large estate, park, yellow fall color.
PROBLEMS: Dutch elm disease, elm leaf beetle, cotton root rot, and lacebugs.
NOTES: Ascending elm is an upright-growing version that was a failure. Neither of these plants is recommended, although I would certainly save any existing ones. Native to the eastern half of the United States.

American Elm

ELM, CEDAR
Ulmus crassifolia
(ULL-mus krass-ih-FOE-lee-uh)

Deciduous—Sun
Ht. 80' Spread 60'
Spacing 20'–40'

HABIT: Upright, moderate growth, yellow/gold fall color, irregular growth pattern, rough-textured leaves.
CULTURE: Any soil, drought tolerant but can stand fairly wet soil also. Can be severely damaged by removing lower limbs.
USES: Shade tree, street tree.
PROBLEMS: Aphids, elm leaf beetle, mildew, mistletoe. Seems to be sensitive to air pollution. Removing lower limbs can stress tree.

NOTES: Referred to as "poor man's live oak." Winged elm (*U. alata*), a close kin, has the same characteristics as cedar elm with the addition of wings on the stems. Native from southern United States to West Texas.

Cedar Elm

ELM, LACEBARK
Drake Elm
Ulmus parvifolia sempervirens
(ULL-mus par-vi-FOE-lee-uh sem-per-VYE-rens)

Deciduous—Sun
Ht. 50' Spread 40'
Spacing 20'–30'

HABIT: Upright and spreading, delicate foliage on limber stems, trunk bark is distinctively mottled. Fall color is so-so yellow.
CULTURE: Easy to grow in most soils, drought tolerant, although cannot tolerate wet soil. Almost evergreen in the Houston area.
USES: Shade tree.
PROBLEMS: Cotton root rot. Very tender bark in early spring just at leaf break.
NOTES: Often confused with Siberian elm (*U. pumila*), which is a trash tree. Sold as Drake elm, evergreen elm, or Chinese elm. Native to China.

EVE'S NECKLACE
Texas Sophora
Sophora affinis
(so-FORE-uh af-FIN-is)

Deciduous—Sun/Shade
Ht. 30' Spread 20'
Spacing 10'–15'

Eve's Necklace

HABIT: Moderately fast-growing legume, upright, usually in the wild as an understory tree. Pink wisteria-like flowers and decorative black beadlike seedpods in fall. Bark, especially new young growth, is green. Yellow fall color.
CULTURE: Easy to grow in most soils, drought tolerant.

50

USES: Small garden tree, specimen, natural settings.
PROBLEMS: Few if any.
NOTES: Excellent small tree for residential gardens. Native to Texas, Arkansas, Oklahoma, and Louisiana.

Fringe Tree

FRINGE TREE

Chinese Fringe Tree
Chionanthus virginicus
(key-oh-NAN-thus ver-JIN-ih-kus)

Deciduous—Part Shade
Ht. 15'–30' Spread 15'–20'
Spacing 10'–25'

HABIT: Lacy, fragrant white flower clusters in spring just before foliage appears and immediately after the dogwoods bloom. Both male and female flowers are beautiful. Female plants have dark blue clusters of berries that ripen in late summer to fall. Gorgeous slow-growing ornamental native tree.
CULTURE: Does best in sandy, acid soils but will grow in soil with a neutral pH—in Houston, for example. Yellow fall color. Moderate water requirements. Can grow in wet soil.
USES: Ornamental understory tree, spring color.
PROBLEMS: Not adapted to alkaline soil.
NOTES: Flowers form on year-old growth, so prune only after blooming. American species does well on moist soils; Chinese species is better on dry soils and really a better choice for Houston.

GINKGO

Maidenhair Tree
Ginkgo biloba
(GINK-o bye-LOBE-uh)

Deciduous—Sun
Ht. 50' Spread 30'
Spacing 20'–40'

HABIT: Unique, open-branching tree with vibrant yellow fall color. Foliage is medium green, fan shaped, and beautiful. Light-color bark and slow growth.
CULTURE: Any well-drained soil. Doesn't like solid rock. Moderate water and fertilization needs. Responds extremely well to the organic program.
USES: Shade tree, fall color, distinctive foliage. Medicinal herb from the foliage helps improve mental functions, according to some research.
PROBLEMS: Female fruit stinks, slow grower.
NOTES: One of the oldest trees on earth and can be found on almost every continent in the world. Largest I've seen is in Frank Lloyd Wright's office garden in Chicago. First identified from fossil records in China.

Ginkgo

Goldenrain Tree

Parsley Hawthorn

GOLDENRAIN TREE

Koelreuteria paniculata
(cole-roo-TEH-ree-ah pan-ik-
you-LAY-tuh)

Deciduous—Sun
Ht. 30' Spread 20'
Spacing 15'–20'

HABIT: Upright and open branching, yellow flowers in summer, decorative pods following.
CULTURE: Easy to grow in any soil, moderately drought tolerant. Does not like heavy fertilization.
USES: Medium-sized shade tree, summer color. Good for hot spots.
PROBLEMS: Few if any, other than relatively short-lived.
NOTES: Ugly duckling when small but develops into a beautiful tree. Native to the Orient. *K. bipinnata*, a close kin, is not as cold hardy but is more heat tolerant.

HAWTHORN, PARSLEY

Parsleyleaf Hawthorn
Crataegus marshallii
(krah-TEEG-us MAR-shul-eye)

Deciduous—Sun/Part Shade
Ht. 25' Spread 25'
Spacing 10'–20'

HABIT: White flowers in spring, delicate parsleylike foliage, and red fruit (haws) in fall. Flaky bark and usually has multiple trunks.
CULTURE: Does best in sandy, acid soil but fairly adaptable elsewhere, drought tolerant.
USES: Understory tree, specimen garden tree.
PROBLEMS: Cedar apple rust, aphids, and other insects. Chlorosis in alkaline soils.
NOTES: Beautiful small tree. Found mostly in higher, well-drained rocky soils. Native to East Texas. Texas hawthorn (*C. texana*) is quite similar.

HICKORY

Carya spp.
(CARE-ee-uh)

Deciduous—Sun
Ht. 50'–140' Spread 30'–50'
Spacing 20'–30'

HABIT: About eight species in Texas, hard to tell apart. They have very similar characteristics and hybridize freely between species. Foliage looks similar to that of pecan, but the leaflets are bigger.
CULTURE: Generally likes moist, acid soils of

East Texas. *C. glabra*, pignut hickory, likes well-drained ridges. *C. texana*, black hickory, likes dry, granite-rock hillsides. *C. ovata*, shagbark hickory, has the sweetest nuts.

USES: Shade tree, edible nuts.

PROBLEMS: Won't grow well in alkaline soils.

NOTES: The state champion 97-foot pignut hickory is in Trinity National Wildlife Refuge near Houston.

Hickory

HOLLY, DECIDUOUS
Ilex decidua
(EYE-lex dih-SID-you-uh)

Deciduous—Sun/Shade
Ht. 20' Spread 15'
Spacing 12'–15'

HABIT: Bushy growth if not trimmed, small leaves, red berries on bare branches all winter long—on female plants only.

CULTURE: Easy to grow in most soils, drought tolerant but tolerant of moist soils.

USES: Winter color, understory tree, specimen garden tree.

PROBLEMS: Suckers from base, buying male plants accidentally.

NOTES: Best to purchase when the berries can be seen on the plant. The male is not worth much unless used for the contrast. Native from southeastern United States to Texas.

Deciduous Holly

HOLLY, 'EAST PALATKA'
Ilex × *attenuata* 'East Palatka'
(EYE-lex ah-ten-you-AY-tuh)

Evergreen—Sun/Part Shade
Ht. 15'–30' Spread 10'–15'
Spacing 8'–10'

HABIT: Terrific large bush or small tree. Upright, moderate growth, graceful open branching. Bright red berries in winter, smooth light bark.

CULTURE: Easy to grow in any soil except solid rock, needs good drainage. Responds very well to the organic program.

USES: Specimen ornamental, evergreen border, small garden tree.

PROBLEMS: Scale, mealybugs, iron deficiency (none serious).

NOTES: Distinguished by one spine on end of leaf rather than several, like 'Savannah' and 'Foster'. All are hybrids of American holly (*I. opaca*).

'East Palatka' Holly

Savannah Holly

Yaupon Holly

Jujube

HOLLY, SAVANNAH
Ilex opaca × *attenuata* 'Savannah'
(EYE-lex o-PAY-kuh)

Evergreen—Sun/Part Shade
Ht. 15'–30' Spread 10'–15'
Spacing 8'–12'

HABIT: Moderate upright and pyramidal growth, with medium green spiny leaves. Lots of red berries in winter.
CULTURE: Easy to grow in any well-drained soil. Turns yellow and chlorotic when fertilized with synthetic salt-based fertilizers.
USES: Small specimen garden tree, border, or evergreen background.
PROBLEMS: Few; leaf miners occasionally.
NOTES: Good small evergreen tree. Is beginning to be used often.

HOLLY, YAUPON
Ilex vomitoria
(EYE-lex vom-ee-TORE-ee-uh)

Evergreen—Sun/Shade
Ht. 20' Spread 20'
Spacing 10'–15'

HABIT: Bushy unless trimmed into tree form. Light-color bark, interesting branching. Red berries in winter on female plants.
CULTURE: Easy to grow in all soils. Drought tolerant but grows much faster when irrigated regularly. Can stand fairly wet soil.
USES: Ornamental understory or specimen tree. Good for courtyards and small garden spaces. Wonderful landscape plant. Birds love this tree.
PROBLEMS: Occasional leaf miners in summer—nothing serious.
NOTES: Native to Central Texas. Weeping yaupon holly has a dramatic overall upright structure with weeping limbs.

JUJUBE
Ziziphus spp.
(ZIZ-ih-fuss)

Deciduous—Sun
Ht. 25'–30' Spread 15'–30'
Spacing 20'–30'

HABIT: Clusters of small yellow flowers in early summer. Shiny, edible, datelike purple-brown fruit in fall. Branches and twigs are spiny, gnarled, zigzagged (hence the name). Glossy dark green leaves.
CULTURE: Slow to moderate growth in almost any soil.
USES: Unique shade tree. Edible and medicinal fruit that tastes like dried apples.
PROBLEMS: Can spread by root sprouts and seeds to become a rather annoying pest.
NOTES: One of the easiest fruit trees to grow.

KIDNEYWOOD, TEXAS

Bee Brush (*Eysenhardtia texana*) Small tree to 15' with a spread of 6'–8'. Deciduous irregularly shaped plant for full sun or light shade. Usually less than 8' tall growing in rocky, calcareous soils. Wonderfully fragrant white to pale yellow flowers; delicate-looking foliage is tangerine scented when bruised. Blooming period begins in the summer, especially after rains; sometimes begins in May and goes through late August or September. Fruit is a small (¼"–⅝") legume containing one seed. Fairly easy to grow in most well-drained soils. Drought tolerant but grows better with adequate moisture. Needs very little fertilizer.

LOCUST, BLACK

(*Robinia pseudoacacia*) Upright and spreading tree to 40', small oval leaflets on large compound leaves; dramatic fragrant white flowers in spring, yellow fall color. Fast-growing but not long-lived. Easy to grow in any soil and drought tolerant. Native to Oklahoma, Arkansas, and east to New York. Has naturalized in Texas. 'Purple Robe' is a dramatic purple-flowering cultivar.

Black Locust

Saucer Magnolia

Saucer Magnolia

Southern Magnolia

MAGNOLIA, SOUTHERN
Magnolia grandiflora
(mag-NOLE-ee-uh gran-dee-FLORE-uh)

Evergreen—Sun
Ht. 60' Spread 30'
Spacing 30'–50'

HABIT: Straight central stem, foliage to ground unless trimmed up. Fibrous, shallow root system. Large white flowers a few at a time in summer.
CULTURE: Relatively easy, although they like sandy, acid soils best. Do not even

try in solid-rock areas. Will grow to 100' in deep sandy soils. Needs lots of room.

USES: Specimen tree for large area.

PROBLEMS: Chlorosis. Difficult to grow anything under this plant. Continuous leaf drop.

NOTES: Native from southeastern United States to East Texas. Saucer magnolia (*M. soulangiana*) is deciduous with pink flowers in spring, grows 20'. Star magnolia (*M. stellata*) has white flowers, is deciduous, and grows to 12'. Both do better with some shade. Many cultivars exist. A good small-leafed variety is 'Little Gem'. Bigleaf magnolia is as dramatic as the name suggests.

Bigleaf Magnolia

MAGNOLIA, BAY

Sweet Bay Magnolia

(*Magnolia virginiana*) Deciduous to semi-evergreen tree to 40', fragrant white flowers, leaves white beneath and beautiful when the wind blows them. Fruits are attractive crimson cones. Likes moist soil. Also called sweet bay, swamp bay, and swamp magnolia.

Bay Magnolia

Chalk Maple

MAPLE, CHALK

White Bark Maple

Acer leucoderme

(A-sir lew-ko-DER-me)

Deciduous—Shade
Ht. 15'–30' Spread 10'–15'
Spacing 10'–15'

HABIT: Small tree with a rounded top and beautiful foliage, golden and red fall color. Small yellow flowers bloom in the spring—usually in April. The fruit, a winged seed, matures in September and is usually heavy and showy. Foliage appears at the same time the flowers emerge and has pale hairs, which give a vel-

vety feel to the underside of the leaves. The mature foliage usually droops.

CULTURE: Easy to grow in any moist soil but adapts to drier situations. Needs very little fertilizer but does respond to good conditions.

USES: Small to medium specimen or small-area shade tree.

PROBLEMS: Few problems exist other than environmental stresses. Under the Basic Organic Program, it should be virtually pest free. Lack of availability in the nursery trade is currently a common problem.

NOTES: This is one of those well-adapted Texas maples that should be used quite a bit more. At the moment, availability at the nurseries is not great. As more people request the tree, availability will increase.

MAPLE, DRUMMOND RED
Red Maple
Acer rubrum
(A-sir ROO-brum)

Deciduous—Sun
Ht. 60'–90' Spread 30'–40'
Spacing 20'–40'

HABIT: Medium to large trees with upright oval crowns. Leaves are usually green above and powdery silver white and hairy underneath. Leaf stems are reddish in the spring. Fall color is red orange to red. Dramatic scarlet winged fruit (samaras) in the spring.
CULTURE: Grows in a wide range of soils but not highly drought tolerant. Best in moist to poorly drained locations. Responds very well to the organic program.
USES: Shade tree.
PROBLEMS: Drought conditions and white rock soils.
NOTES: Also known as scarlet maple, swamp maple, soft maple, Carolina red maple, and water maple. This and Trident maple are the two best maples for Houston.

MAPLE, JAPANESE
Acer palmatum
(A-sir pal-MAY-tum)

Deciduous—Shade/Part Shade
Ht. 6'–20' Spread 10'–20'
Spacing 10'–15'

HABIT: Beautiful spreading branches on various-sized varieties, some tall, others dwarf; some red, others green.
CULTURE: Relatively easy to grow in any soil, normal water and fertilization. Best in light shade. Plant high—make sure the root flare is above ground.
USES: Specimen garden tree, understory tree, year-round color. Smaller varieties are good in pots.
PROBLEMS: Delicate foliage will sometimes burn in heat of summer—not harmful.
NOTES: The green species is the largest-growing and toughest. The green-leafed varieties and cultivars are the easiest to grow and have terrific fall color. 'Dissectum' is the dwarf lacy leaf, and 'Coral Bark' has bright red stems in winter. There are hundreds of choices, even variegated forms. Over 400 varieties exist. Native to Japan.

Japanese Maple—'Orangeola'

Japanese Maple—'Crimson Queen'

Southern Sugar Maple

MAPLE, SOUTHERN SUGAR

Florida Maple
Acer barbatum
(A-sir bar-BAY-tum)

Deciduous—Sun
Ht. 30'–80' Spread 30'–60'
Spacing 25'–30'

HABIT: Beautiful upright-growing tree with fall leaf color that ranges from scarlet and crimson to orange and old gold. It is smaller and more heat tolerant than true sugar maple (*A. saccharum* var. *saccharum*) but does well from Dallas to Houston. Size depends on health and depth of soil.

CULTURE: Tolerates most soils, wet and dry weather conditions, high winds, and other environmental stresses. Does best in healthy well-drained soils. Likes some afternoon shade.

USES: Interesting shade tree with striking fall color—sometimes.

PROBLEMS: It is very sensitive to spray drift of 2,4-D and other toxic herbicides, as are most trees.

NOTES: A good maple to try.

MAPLE, TRIDENT

Acer buergerianum
(A-sir ber-jair-AY-num)

Deciduous—Part Sun/Part Shade
Ht. 30'–45' Spread 25'
Spacing 20'–30'

HABIT: Rounded crown, with beautiful 3-inch-wide trilobed leaves, glossy green above and paler underneath, which turn various shades of red, orange, and yellow in the fall. Flowers are bright yellow and showy in the spring. Spreading growth and multiple stems but can be trained to a single trunk. Moderate growth rate, attractive orange-brown peeling bark.

CULTURE: Easy maintenance—water moderately in summer, easing off in winter. Normal fertilization needed.

USES: Popular as a patio or street tree and is also highly valued as a bonsai subject, due to its small three-lobed leaves; a readily thickening trunk; and thick, gnarly roots that adapt well to root-over-rock style.

PROBLEMS: Branches are somewhat brittle.

NOTES: One of the best maples for the Gulf Coast.

Trident Maple

OAK, BUR
Quercus macrocarpa
(KWER-kus mack-row-CAR-puh)

Deciduous—Sun
Ht. 80' Spread 80'
Spacing 30'–50'

HABIT: Majestic spreading shade tree, large leaves up to 1', golf-ball-size acorns, so-so yellow fall color. Thick, corklike stems, branches, and trunk. Fast-growing quality oak that can reach 150'.
CULTURE: Easy to grow once established in any well-drained soil, including solid-rock areas. Drought tolerant. Grows almost anywhere in the United States.
USES: Handsome, hardy, and fast-growing shade tree.
PROBLEMS: Lacebugs and aphids when in stress.
NOTES: Possibly my favorite shade tree. One of the longest-lived oaks. Also called mossy oak or cup oak. Native to Texas, Oklahoma, and eastern United States.

Bur Oak

OAK, CANBY
Quercus canbyi
(KWER-kus CAN-bee-eye)

Semi-evergreen—Sun
Ht. 50' Spread 30'–40'
Spacing 20'–30'

HABIT: Upright red oak–like tree with a very neat appearance. It is usually completely evergreen in Houston and nearby areas.

CULTURE: Easy to grow in most any soil. Should be used much more in Texas.
USES: Shade tree.
PROBLEMS: None serious if planted properly.
NOTES: Beautiful tree that should be used much more. Chisos oak is a similar tree. Leaf size varies greatly. Some are evergreen; some are semi-evergreen and hold red foliage most of the winter.

Canby Oak

OAK, CHINKAPIN
Chinquapin Oak
Quercus muhlenbergii
(KWER-kus mew-lin-BERG-ee-eye)

Deciduous—Sun
Ht. 80' Spread 80'
Spacing 30'–50'

HABIT: Irregularly spreading, relatively fast growth, dark purple acorns, yellow-brown fall color. Some selections have red fall color as shown here.
CULTURE: Any soil, very sensitive to poor drainage, drought tolerant.
USES: Shade tree.
PROBLEMS: Wet feet and transplant difficulties.
NOTES: Easily confused with chestnut oak, which will not grow here. Chestnut

Chinkapin Oak

oak has rounded lobes in contrast to the chinkapin's sharp-pointed edges. Native to Texas, Oklahoma, and eastern United States.

OAK, DURAND
Bigelow Oak
Quercus sinuata var. *sinuata*
(KWER-kus sin-you-AY-tuh)

Deciduous—Sun
Ht. 60' Spread 40'
Spacing 20'–50'

HABIT: Upright, open branching, dense rounded top, smallish leaves with rounded lobes. Handsome tree with reddish fall color.
CULTURE: Easy to grow in any well-drained soil. Drought tolerant and doesn't mind rocky soil.
USES: Shade tree.
PROBLEMS: Few if any. Not easily available in the nursery trade at this time.
NOTES: Bigelow oak (*Quercus sinuata* var. *breviloba*) is a small-growing close kin. Bigelow is native to the North Texas area. Durand is native from Waco to Central Texas, but the 75-foot national champion is in the Trinity National Wildlife Refuge near Houston.

OAK, LACEY
Smokey Oak, Canyon Oak, Rich Oak
Quercus laceyi (syn. *Q. glaucoides*)
(KWER-kus LACE-ee-eye)

Deciduous—Sun
Ht. 25'–35' Spread 15'–20'
Spacing 15'–20'

Lacey Oak

HABIT: Beautiful small- to medium-sized tree with blue-green mature foliage and peach-colored new growth and fall color.
CULTURE: Easy to grow and adapts to many soils, from sand to heavy clays.
USES: Small shade tree for extremely well-drained or dry areas.
PROBLEMS: It lacks availability in the trade. Not able to stand wet soil continuously.
NOTES: MUST HAVE EXCELLENT DRAINAGE. The leaves are quite small in comparison to other oaks. Lacey oak is a trouble-free tree that should be used much more in the landscape. Not recommended for Houston by everyone.

OAK, LAUREL
(*Quercus laurifolia*) Also called Darlington oak, diamondleaf oak, swamp laurel oak, laurel leaf oak, obtusa oak. Semi-evergreen shade tree similar to willow oak but has wider leaves, over 1" long, often lobed on young trees. Native to moist areas in a limited range in East Texas. Not good in alkaline soils. Will be somewhat hard to find in nurseries. This is a poor alternative to live oak.

Laurel Oak

OAK, LIVE
Coastal Live Oak
Quercus virginiana
(KWER-kus ver-jin-ee-AN-uh)

Evergreen—Sun
Ht. 40'–50' Spread 40'–50'
Spacing 40'

HABIT: Spreading evergreen shade tree. Small glossy leaves vary in shape and size. Single and multiple trunks. Black acorns. Extremely dramatic and beautiful tree with a wide or graceful head. Large limbs tend to dip and sweep to the ground. On some of the most beautiful live oaks, the limbs actually rest on the ground. It is an arborilogical crime to prune away these wonderful limbs.
CULTURE: Live oak is easy to establish and easy to grow but is a relatively high-maintenance tree because it's dropping something year-round—leaves, flowers, or acorns. Most people have the misconception that it is a clean tree because it is evergreen. It responds well to ample moisture and fertilizer, but overfertilization can bring on various pest problems, including root fungal diseases.

Live Oak

PROBLEMS: Aphids, galls, oak wilt. Most all diseases can be controlled by improving the immune system of the tree. Use the Sick Tree Treatment to improve the health of the soil and the root system of the tree.
NOTES: Live oaks are curiously tolerant to construction around their root systems. Looks its worst in spring when new leaves are kicking off the old leaves.

OAK, MEXICAN
Monterrey Oak
Quercus polymorpha
(KWER-kus poly-MORE-fuh)

Deciduous to Semi-deciduous—Sun
Ht. 40'–60' Spread 30'–40'
Spacing 30'

HABIT: Monterrey oak is a deciduous to evergreen medium-sized shade tree that has thick, rounded dark green leaves. It has little to no fall color.
CULTURE: Easy to grow in well-drained soil.
USES: Unusual shade tree.
PROBLEMS: It has few problems other than possible freeze damage in the far northern part of the state.
NOTES: Beavers seem to love chewing on this tree—I learned that the hard way. Monterrey oak is said to be a trademarked name owned by Lone Star Growers of San Antonio. Evergreen in the southern tip of Texas and in Mexico.

Mexican Oak

Texas Red Oak

OAK, WILLOW

Pin Oak, Swamp Willow Oak
Quercus phellos
(KWER-kus FELL-oss)

Deciduous—Sun
Ht. 80'–100' Spread 40'–60'
Spacing 30'–50'

HABIT: Grows in the deep, sandy, acid, moist soil of East Texas. Can grow in clays or loams and is often seen along stream bottoms and frequently flooded drainage ways. It will grow in deep clay soils but not above white limestone rock. Pyramidal when young but spreads into a rounded crown with age. Narrow, delicate leaves. Yellow fall color.
CULTURE: Needs moist, acid, sandy soils. Will not grow as well in the alkaline soils, especially where white limestone is present. Requires plenty of moisture but minimal fertilization.
USES: Shade tree.
PROBLEMS: Nutrient deficiency and chlorosis can result from its being planted in the improper soil.
NOTES: Its acorns are a favorite of several forms of wildlife. Willow oak is easily confused with its close relatives laurel oak and water oak.

Wild Olive

OLIVE, WILD

Cordia boissieri
(KOR-dee-uh bois-see-ERR-ee)

Evergreen—Sun
Ht. 15'–25' Spread 10'–15'
Spacing 10'–15'

HABIT: Grows in the far southern tip of Texas in the counties along the Rio Grande.

Texas Olive

Adaptable as far north as San Antonio but will freeze to the ground there in harsh winters. It is a rounded evergreen tree with dramatic 2" hibiscus-like white flowers and velvety leaves.
CULTURE: Needs a lot of water to get established but is drought tolerant once established.
USES: Small dramatic specimen tree. Excellent butterfly attractor.
PROBLEMS: Freeze damage can occur anywhere north of San Antonio.
NOTES: Fruit is reported to be sweet, pulpy, and edible, although warnings exist that it can cause dizziness when eaten in excess. This is the beautiful tree just to the left of the front door of the Alamo in San Antonio.

ORANGE, TRIFOLIATE

(*Poncirus trifoliata*) Deciduous well-armed citrus with hard, bitter, inedible yellow-orange fruit. Easy to grow just about anywhere. Good as an impenetrable hedge or as rootstock for other citrus trees. Ugly and thorny but makes a great barrier plant.

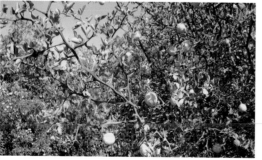

Trifoliate Orange

ORCHID TREE

Bauhinia congesta (syn. *B. lunarioides*)
(baw-HIN-ee-uh kun-JESS-tuh)

Deciduous—Sun/Part Shade
Ht. 6'–10' Spread 6'–10'
Spacing 10'–12'

Orchid Tree

HABIT: Southern part of the state. Can stand temperatures down to 10°F and does well in the Austin, Houston, and San Antonio climates. Usually multitrunked and deciduous. Beautiful light green leaves that are divided at the base into two leaflets. Showy flowers in the spring and yellow fall color.
CULTURE: Will grow in a wide range of well-drained soils, from clay and rocky soils to sandy loams, if protected from harsh winter temperatures. Seems to like limestone conditions. Drought tolerant and needs little fertilizer or pest control.
USES: It is best used as an understory tree.
PROBLEMS: Freeze damage is possible in the northern half of the state.
NOTES: Orchid tree is a terrific specimen tree. Even if you live in the northern part of the state, try it in pots and move it to a protected area in the winter.

PALM, TEXAS

Sabal Palm
Sabal mexicana (syn. *S. texana*)
(SAY-ball mex-ee-KAH-nuh)

Evergreen—Sun/Part Shade
Ht. 20'–50' Spread 5'–8'
Spacing 8'–10'

Sabal Palm

HABIT: Native to the southern tip of Texas but will adapt to landscape sites as far north as the Dallas/Fort Worth area. Classic palm look with a single trunk and large fan-shaped leaves forming a rounded crown. For eight to ten years the tree grows into a large clump before the trunk starts to appear at the base. Leaves have curving ribs in the center and a tangle of leaf threads. Leaf stems are smooth (no teeth). White flowers in midsummer, followed by olive-size black berrylike fruit. *S. palmetto*, or cabbage palm, has a smaller crown and pea-size fruit.

Needle Palm

Windmill Palm

65

Pindo Palm

CULTURE: Slow-growing with a large root system, which makes it rather hard to transplant after the plant is large. Easy to grow in a wide range of soils and fairly drought tolerant. Very salt tolerant.
USES: Evergreen specimen tree.
PROBLEMS: Freeze damage occurs in the far northern part of the state.
NOTES: Texas palm is the only tree-size palm native to Texas and the best choice to use. *S. minor* is the Texas fan palm, or palmetto. It only grows 4'–6' and does not form a trunk. Other adapted palms for the area include fan palm, windmill palm, pindo palm, needle palm, sago palm (not a real palm), pigmy date, Washington palm, queen palm, and date palm.

PARASOL TREE
Chinese Varnish Tree
Firmiana simplex
(fir-me-AN-uh SIM-plex)

Deciduous—Sun
Ht. 40' Spread 30'
Spacing 20'–30'

HABIT: Fast-growing, upright, smooth green bark when young, huge leaves, thick stems.
CULTURE: Very easy, maybe too easy, to grow in most any soil, relatively drought tolerant, average water and fertilizer needs.
USES: Shade tree, conversation piece.
PROBLEMS: Coarse-looking, weak wood. Will be found popping up all over your landscape.
NOTES: Native to China and Japan.

Edible Peach

PEACH, EDIBLE
The best peaches for the Gulf Coast are those with low chilling requirements, such as Early Amber—300 hrs. of chilling, yellow meat; Mid-Pride—250 hrs., clingstone, yellow meat, very good flavor; Chelena—175 hrs., clingstone, yellow meat; Tropic Snow—200 hrs., white meat, excellent flavor; Scarlet Robe—600 hrs., yellow meat, excellent flavor; Red Baron—650 hrs., freestone, yellow meat; Tex Royal—600 hrs., excellent flavor; Novark—550 hrs., white meat, Belle of Georgia seedling.

PEACH, FLOWERING
(*Prunus persica*) Deciduous 10'–15' tall ornamental tree with early spring flowers of all colors. Easy to grow in any soil, relatively drought tolerant. Flowers occur on second year's growth, so prune carefully.

Flowering Peach

PECAN
Carya illinoinensis
(CARE-ee-uh ill-e-noy-NEN-sis)

Deciduous—Sun
Ht. 100' Spread 100'
Spacing 30'–50'

HABIT: Irregularly spreading, extremely graceful, yellow fall color, very long-lived, deeply rooted.

CULTURE: Easy to grow pretty much anywhere.

USES: Shade tree, pecan crop.

PROBLEMS: Worst is webworms, which is mainly an aesthetic problem. Pecan nut casebearers, but they are easily controlled with trichogramma wasp releases starting at leaf emergence. Somewhat messy most of the time but well worth it.

NOTES: Great choice for State Tree. The native varieties make better landscape trees than hybrids developed for soft-shell pecan crops. Native to North America.

Pecan

PERSIMMON, COMMON
Diospyros virginiana
(dye-OS-pear-us ver-jin-ee-AN-uh)

Deciduous—Sun
Ht. 60' Spread 30'
Spacing 20'–40'

HABIT: Yellow fall color; dark, deeply fissured bark. Shiny foliage that gracefully droops. 1" orange fruit matures after first frost.

CULTURE: Easy, any soil, drought tolerant.

USES: Shade tree.

PROBLEMS: Webworms, messy fruit.

NOTES: This tree's few problems don't keep it from being an excellent shade tree. Japanese varieties are smaller plants but have large fruit the size of apples. Wooden golf clubs were made from persimmon. Native to Texas and the eastern United States.

Common Persimmon

Japanese Persimmon

PERSIMMON, TEXAS
Diospyros texana
(dye-OS-pear-us tex-AN-uh)

Deciduous—Sun/Part Shade
Ht. 20' Spread 12'
Spacing 12'–15'

HABIT: Trunks and branches resemble crape myrtle. Small leaves, insignificant fall color. Slow-growing. Small leathery leaves. 1" fruit turns black in fall.

CULTURE: Easy to grow in most soils, drought tolerant. Can grow easily in rocky areas.

USES: Ornamental garden tree, decorative bark.

PROBLEMS: Few if any.

NOTES: Native to South and Central Texas.

67   *Texas Persimmon*

Sweetgum

USES: Specimen garden tree, backdrop.
PROBLEMS: Chlorosis and foliage burn in shallow soils.
NOTES: An ancient tree native to China and Japan. Distinctive, durable tree that definitely should be used more.

SWEETGUM
Liquidambar styraciflua
(lik-wid-AM-bur sty-ruh-SIFF-lou-uh)

Deciduous—Sun
Ht. 70' Spread 30'
Spacing 20'–30'

HABIT: Vertical, cone-shaped, spreading with age. Red, salmon, orange, and yellow fall color. Stiff branching. Round spiny seedpods.
CULTURE: Needs deep soil and prefers sandy, acid conditions—hates solid rock. Quite easy to transplant if given ample water.
USES: Shade tree, great fall color.
PROBLEMS: Chlorosis; dry, rocky soil.
NOTES: Native to East Texas and other sandy-soil areas. Will grow much larger in sandy, acid soils. Needs lots of water and acidifiers in alkaline soils. Cultivars include 'Palo Alto' and 'Burgundy'. They have excellent fall color but are not adapted to North or Central Texas.

SYCAMORE, MEXICAN

(*Plantanus mexicana*) Native to northeastern Mexico. It is a large tree, reaching 60' tall or more. The lobed leaves are also large at up to 8" wide and are smooth green on the top but cottony white to silvery below. It has attractive exfoliating bark that is white in winter. It is well adapted to dry, rocky alkaline soils but adapts to moist soils as well. As opposed to the native sycamore (*P. occidentalis*), Mexican sycamore is a good choice for the Gulf Coast due to its tolerance of various soils.

TEXAS MOUNTAIN LAUREL
Sophora secundiflora
(so-FORE-uh se-kune-dih-FLORE-uh)

Evergreen—Sun/Part Shade
Ht. 20' Spread 10'
Spacing 8'–15'

Texas Mountain Laurel

HABIT: Slow-growing, dense foliage, bushy unless trimmed into tree form. Fragrant, purple, wisteria-like flowers in spring. They actually smell like grape soda.
CULTURE: Any well-drained soil. Moderate to low water and feeding requirements.
USES: Specimen ornamental tree or large shrub.

Drought-tolerant gardens. Can be grown in containers.

PROBLEMS: Winter damage in the northern parts of the state.

NOTES: Great in Central to South Texas. Native to southwestern United States, Texas, and Mexico.

Tulip Tree

TULIP TREE

Tulip Poplar, Yellow Poplar, Whitewood

Liriodendron tulipifera

(lir-ee-oh-DEN-dron too-li-PIF-err-uh)

Deciduous—Sun
Ht. 70' Spread 40'
Spacing 30'–40'

HABIT: Straight trunk, smooth bark, leaves shaped like tulips, yellow fall color. Interesting flowers in late spring but sometimes hard to see.

CULTURE: Any deep, well-drained soil. Does not like rock. High water requirement in heat of summer.

USES: Shade tree.

PROBLEMS: Leaf drop in mid to late summer.

NOTES: The only poplar that I recommend. Native to midwestern, northeastern, and southeastern United States.

Rusty Blackhaw Viburnum

VIBURNUM, RUSTY BLACKHAW

Black Haw

Viburnum rufidulum

(Vi-BUR-num rue-FID-you-lum)

Deciduous—Sun/Shade
Ht. 20'–40' Spread 20'
Spacing 10'–20'

HABIT: Shrubby tree, glossy leaves, white flower clusters in spring, reddish fall color, blue-black berries in late summer.

CULTURE: Easy to grow in most soils, extremely drought tolerant.

USES: Specimen garden tree, understory tree, background mass planting.

PROBLEMS: Few if any—practically maintenance free. However, not easy to find in the nursery trade at this point.

NOTES: Great little tree. Native to Texas and Oklahoma.

VITEX

Chaste Tree, Fly Tree, Indian Spice, Sage Tree, Hemp Monk's Pepper Tree

Vitex agnus-castus

(VI-teks AG-nus-CAS-tus)

Deciduous—Sun
Ht. 20' Spread 25'
Spacing 15'–20'

HABIT: Called Lilac Chaste tree also. Spreading, usually multistemmed, brittle wood, not long-lived. Purple or white flowers in early summer. Nicely textured foliage.

CULTURE: Easy to grow in any soil, drought tolerant.

Vitex

Black Walnut

USES: Summer flowers, foliage texture.

PROBLEMS: Short life, freeze damage.

NOTES: Native to Europe and Asia. Should not be used as a primary tree but rather as a secondary tree for special interest. 'Montrose Purple' is a large-flowering cultivar to try.

WALNUT, BLACK

Juglans nigra

(JEW-gluns NYE-gruh)

Deciduous—Sun

Ht. 50' Spread 50'

Spacing 20'–50'

HABIT: Open-branching character, large distinctive leaves with evenly sized and arranged leaflets on each side of stem. Yellow fall color. Dark bark. Moderate to slow growth.

CULTURE: Likes deep soil, good drainage. Although tolerates alkaline soil, likes a more neutral soil.

USES: Shade tree, nut crop.

PROBLEMS: Roots give off a toxin harmful to some other plants. Nut is mostly structure but has delicious meat.

NOTES: Native to the southern United States.

Wax Myrtle

WAX MYRTLE

Myrica cerifera

(MY-ruh-kuh sir-RIFF-ih-ruh)

Evergreen—Sun to Part Shade

Ht. 15' Spread 10'

Spacing 8'–12'

HABIT: Moderately fast-growing, spreading, with many small medium green leaves, blue-gray berries in fall. Aromatic foliage dotted above and below.

CULTURE: Easy, any soil, drought tolerant.

USES: Specimen garden tree, evergreen background. Good alternative to tree yaupon.

PROBLEMS: Brittle wood, suckers.

NOTES: Birds like the berries. Dwarf wax myrtle (*M. pusilla*) is also available. Native to the southern states and the eastern half of the United States.

Desert Willow

WILLOW, DESERT

Chilopsis linearis

(KY-lop-sis lin-ee-ERR-is)

Deciduous—Sun

Ht. 30' Spread 25'

Spacing 15'–20'

HABIT: Open branching; delicate foliage; lavender, pink, or white orchidlike blossoms in summer. No fall color to speak of.

CULTURE: Easy to grow in any soil, drought tolerant. Does better with more water.

USES: Specimen garden tree, summer color.

PROBLEMS: Brittle wood and a little wild-looking for some gardens.

NOTES: 'Bubba' is a popular variety.

WITCH HAZEL

Hamamelis virginiana
(ha-ma-MAY-liss ver-jin-ee-AN-uh)

Deciduous—Sun/Part Shade
Ht. 10'–20' Spread 8'–10'
Spacing 8'–10'

Witch Hazel

HABIT: Small, open-growing tree. Foliage and flowers are distinctive, and the yellow fall color is usually quite good. Golden yellow flowers bloom in the fall and winter after the leaves have fallen. Flowers of some species have a red or purple cast at the base. Fruit and flowers form simultaneously. Fruit ripens in the second season.

CULTURE: Easy to grow in various well-drained soils. It works very well as an understory plant but can take full sun as well.

USES: Interesting small tree with herbal uses.

PROBLEMS: Few exist, other than scarce availability in the nursery trade.

NOTES: Wonderful little tree that should be planted more often. The name comes from the fact that dousers, or diviners, like to use this plant for finding water. The seeds are edible, and the leaves are used in herb teas. The seeds are also excellent bird food.

EASY REFERENCE FOR TREES

EVERGREEN

Anacua
Camphor tree
Cedar
Cherry Laurel
Clethera
Holly
Magnolia
Oak, live
Palm
Pine
Texas Mountain Laurel
Wax Myrtle

FALL/WINTER BERRIES

Dogwood
Holly
Viburnum, rusty blackhaw
Wax Myrtle

FLOWERING TREES

Bird of Paradise
Buckeye
Catalpa
Cherry, black
Cherry Laurel
Citrus
Crabapple
Crape myrtle
Dogwood
Eve's necklace
Fringe tree
Goldenrain tree
Hawthorn
Magnolia
Olive, wild
Orchid tree
Peach
Plum
Redbud

Texas Kidneywood
Tulip tree
Viburnum
Vitex
Willow, desert

YELLOW FALL COLOR

Ash
Black Cherry
Buckeye, Mexican
Crape myrtle—white
Elm
Ginkgo
Goldenrain tree
Hickory
Maple
Oak, bur
Pecan
Persimmon
Pistache, Chinese
Redbud
Sweetgum
Tulip tree
Walnut
Witch Hazel

ORANGE FALL COLOR

Ash, Texas
Maple, Japanese
Plum, Mexican

RED FALL COLOR

Black Gum
Crape myrtle—red, pink, purple
Cypress
Dogwood
Maple
Oak, Texas red
Pistache, Chinese
Sweetgum

DO NOT PLANT

Ash, Arizona
Boxelder
Cottonwood
Elm, Siberian
Hackberry
Locust, honey
Maple, silver
Mimosa
Pear, Bradford
Pine, Mondell
Poplars
Sycamore
Tallow, Chinese
Willow, weeping

ABELIA

Abelia grandiflora
(ah-BEE-li-uh gran-dee-FLORE-uh)

Evergreen—Sun/Part Shade
Ht. 6'–8' Spread 6'–8'
Spacing 3'–6'

HABIT: Summer-flowering shrub with tiny white or pink flowers. New growth in long shoots, bronze foliage color.
CULTURE: Very easy to grow in any soil, drought tolerant. Extensive bed preparation not necessary.
USES: Boundary hedge, screen, barrier. Dwarf varieties are good for mass plantings. Long-lasting summer color.
PROBLEMS: Few; plant looks bad when sheared into hedge.
NOTES: Dwarf varieties (3'–5' in height) are available that are suited to smaller gardens: 'Sherwood', 'Prostrata', and 'Edward Goucher'. Abelia is native to Asia.

Abelia

AGARITA

Agarito, Yellow Bells
(*Berberis trifoliata*) Texas native evergreen that is well armed with spiny leaves. It is a slow-growing shrub with brilliant yellow fragrant flowers in the spring, followed by delicious bright red berries. Can be pruned into a thick low hedge, drought tolerant. Must have well-drained soil. Attracts beneficial insects.

AGAVE

Century Plant
(*Agave* spp.) Evergreen specimen plants that grow in many sizes in full sun. Flower stalks get much taller. Very drought tolerant. Sharp spines. All varieties live a long time but die after flowering. Some types are native to Texas.

ALTHEA

Rose of Sharon
Hibiscus syriacus
(Hi-BIS-kus si-ri-AH-kus)

Deciduous—Sun/Part Shade
Ht. 10'–15' Spread 8'–10'
Spacing 8'–10'

Agave

HABIT: Summer-flowering shrub, upright growth. Bare branches in winter. Flower colors are many. Yellow fall color.
CULTURE: Easy to grow in any soil, fairly drought tolerant.

American Beautyberry

Star Anise

Aralia

Aspidistra

USES: Summer flowers.

PROBLEMS: Cotton root rot, aphids. Poorly draining soil will be the end of this plant.

NOTES: Should always be used with evergreens, since it is so homely in the winter. Native to Asia.

AMERICAN BEAUTYBERRY

Callicarpa americana
(kal-ih-KAR-puh uh-mair-ih-KAY-nuh)

Deciduous—Sun/Shade
Ht. 4'–8' Spread 5'–8'
Spacing 3'–5'

HABIT: Sprawling native shrub with insignificant pink flowers in spring. Has extremely showy purple berries in fall that last into the winter.

CULTURE: Well-drained soil is important, but it adapts to any soil type. Very easy to grow but not as drought tolerant as other native shrubs.

USES: Free-form shrub or mass planting. Fall berry color.

PROBLEMS: Few if any.

NOTES: Versatile, carefree plant. Does not work well for cutting—berries fall off. White-berried plants are available. Native from eastern United States to Texas.

ANISE

Star Anise, Florida Anise, Purple Anise, Stink-Bush
(*Illicium floridanum*) Evergreen shrub that can grow 8 feet high and 6 feet wide. It usually grows in dense thickets along stream banks and moist woods. Reddish star-shaped flowers and long, leathery leaves.

ARALIA

Fatsia japonica
(FAT-si-uh juh-PON-ih-kuh)

Evergreen—Shade
Ht. 4'–6' Spread 4'–6'
Spacing 3'–4'

HABIT: Single stem, large tropical-looking leaves, rounded overall shape.

CULTURE: Needs well-prepared bed and good drainage.

USES: Shade gardens, Oriental gardens, tropical effects, coarse texture.

PROBLEMS: Aphids on new growth.

NOTES: Native to Japan.

ASPIDISTRA

Cast Iron Plant
Aspidistra elatior
(as-pi-DIS-tra ee-LAY-she-or)

Evergreen—Shade
Ht. 24" Spread 24"
Spacing 18"

HABIT: Dark green large-leafed foliage plant. Leaves sprout from the ground. Spreads by rhizomes.

CULTURE: Easy to grow in any well-drained soil. Needs shade and plenty of water.

USES: Tall ground cover, coarse texture, low-light area. Container plant.

PROBLEMS: Edges of foliage get ragged, especially in windy areas. Grasshoppers occasionally. Full sun and harsh cold turn the leaves brown.

NOTES: Called cast iron plant and barroom plant because of its toughness. Native to Japan.

AUCUBA

Evergreen—Shade

Aucuba japonica
(ah-CUBE-uh juh-PON-ih-kuh)

Ht. 5'–6' Spread 5'–6'
Spacing 3'

HABIT: Upright growth on thick green stems. Yellow spots on long oval leaves.
CULTURE: Shade, moist soil, and good drainage. Full sun will burn leaf edges black.
USES: Background, coarse texture, screen or accent plant.
PROBLEMS: Scale, nematodes, mealybugs, spider mites—although none of these are serious.
NOTES: Also available in green and dwarf forms. Judy still does not like the spotty ones, but I do. Native to Japan.

Aucuba

Deciduous Azalea

Azalea 'Encore'

AZALEA

Evergreen—Shade / Part Shade

Rhododendron spp.
(row-doe-DEN-dron)

Ht. 3'–6' Spread 3'–6'
Spacing 3'–6'

HABIT: Fibrous-rooted shrubs with spectacular spring colors of red, white, pink, lavender, and all sorts of combinations. Some varieties have attractive evergreen foliage; others are deciduous.
CULTURE: Must be grown in special beds of mostly organic material—half compost and half fine cedar or coconut fiber is a good mixture.
USES: Evergreen hedge or mass, spring color.
PROBLEMS: Summer heat, chlorosis, poor drainage, scale, and spider mites.
NOTES: Encore azaleas are the latest rage because they bloom more than just in the spring. 'Jennifer' and 'Fashion' are also repeat bloomers. Huge numbers of species, varieties, and cultivars are native to various parts of the world. The southern Indicas are tough staples of Houston gardens.

Bamboo

BAMBOO

Bambusa spp.
(bam-BEW-suh)

Evergreen—Sun/Part Shade
Ht. 2'–30' Spread unlimited
Spacing 2'–4'

HABIT: Giant varieties and low-growing ground covers; most bamboos spread like grasses. New sprouts come up once per year in the spring.
CULTURE: Best in partial shade, any soil, no special needs.
USES: Evergreen background, container plant.
PROBLEMS: Spreads and invades other plants. Some varieties will freeze in winter.
NOTES: Spreading can be controlled by kicking over the shoots just as they emerge in the spring. Clumping varieties are available and much less trouble to control. The best choices are 'Alphonse', 'Karr', 'Giant Timber', and 'Budda Belly'. Native to Asia.

BANANA

Musa spp.
(MEW-suh)

Perennial—Sun
Ht. 5'–20' Spread 5'–10'
Spacing 5'–10'

HABIT: All species have thick stems and spread by suckers to form clumps. Large, heavy red or purple flower clusters, followed by edible bananas. Also grows well in greenhouses.

CULTURE: In cooler parts of the state, protect in winter by cutting off the top and putting a thick mulch layer over the stump. If the roots don't stay too wet and rot, the plant will return in the spring.
PROBLEMS: Freeze damage in the northern half of the state, but no problem in the Houston area. Huge leaves are easily torn by the wind.
NOTES: Pieces of banana leaves and stalk are said to repel fleas. The decorative red-leaf varieties are not true bananas.

Banana

BANANA SHRUB

Skinner's Banana Shrub
(*Michelia skinneriana*) Evergreen, 10'–12' large shrub or small tree with attractive dark green glossy foliage and unique banana yellow flowers with a wonderful banana scent. Unique plant that blooms spring, summer, and fall in full sun. Best used as an understory plant but needs plenty of light.

Banana Shrub

BARBADOS CHERRY
Manzanita
Malpighia glabra
(mal-PIG-ee-uh GLAY-bruh)

Evergreen (mostly)—Sun/Part Shade
Ht. 7'–9' Spread 4'–5'
Spacing 3'–5'

HABIT: Small-leafed semi-evergreen shrub. Pale pink and white flowers, followed by cherry-red berries that birds love.
CULTURE: Native to South Texas. Easy to grow with average water and feeding. Responds well to healthy organic beds.
USES: Hedge, specimen, mass planting. Fruit is edible and high in vitamin C.
PROBLEMS: Very few when grown under the organic program.
NOTES: Dwarf variety 'Nana' is also available. Its height is 3'–4'.

Barbados Cherry

BAY
Sweet Bay
Laurus nobilis
(LAR-us NO-bi-lis)

Evergreen—Sun
Ht. 30' Spread 5'–20'
Spacing 5'–10'

HABIT: Bushlike upright evergreen with small creamy flowers in late spring, followed by shiny black berries.
CULTURE: Easy to grow in almost any situation. Does well in pots or in beds.
USES: Flavoring for many foods and teas. Container plant, potpourri, wreaths. Fruit oil is used in making soap. Cut foliage is good for indoor arrangements. Excellent evergreen landscape plant. Can be kept sheared as a hedge.
PROBLEMS: Few other than freeze damage in severe winters.
HARVEST: Collect the evergreen leaves year-round and use fresh or store the dried leaves in glass containers.
NOTES: Mine has been outdoors for over fifteen years and is over 15' tall.

Bay

BOTTLEBRUSH
Callistemon citrinus
(kal-LIS-ta-mon ki-TREE-nus)

Evergreen—Sun
Ht. 8'–12' Spread 4'–8'
Spacing 4'–5'

HABIT: Showy red brushlike flowers in spring, sporadic through summer.
CULTURE: Large upright-growing shrub with red flowers throughout the growing season. Long, slender medium green leaves.
USES: Colorful hedge or screen plant for the South.

79

Boxwood

Carolina Buckthorn

PROBLEMS: Freeze damage in most of Texas. Not reliably hardy above Houston.
NOTES: 'Little John' is the terrific dwarf form. 'Hannah Ray' is also good.

BOXWOOD

(*Buxus microphylla*) Evergreen shrub for sun or part shade that has been used a lot in Houston as a border, low hedge, or foundation planting. I'm not a big fan. Dwarf yaupon is a better choice.

BUCKTHORN, CAROLINA
Indian Cherry
Rhamnus caroliniana
(RAM-nus kar-oh-lin-ee-AN-uh)

Deciduous—Sun/Part Shade
Ht. 15'–26' Spread 15'
Spacing 4'–10'

HABIT: Bushy shrub or small tree. Large glossy leaves, yellow-orange fall color, red berries in late summer turning black in fall. Can grow to 30'.
CULTURE: Easy in any soil with good drainage. Drought tolerant.
USES: Specimen understory plant, ornamental tree, background plant. Good plant for attracting birds.
PROBLEMS: Few if any.
NOTES: Also called Indian cherry, this is a beautiful plant that should certainly be used more.

BUTTERFLY BUSH

Summer Lilac
Buddleia spp.
(BUD-lee-uh)

Deciduous—Sun/Part Shade
Ht. 3'–8' Spread 4'–6'
Spacing 4'–6'

HABIT: Long clusters of fragrant flowers in many colors, mostly in July and August. Arching, open-branching woody growth, thinly foliated. Blooms in spring on second year's growth.
CULTURE: Drought tolerant. Easy to grow in well-prepared beds. Prune after flowers have faded.
USES: Summer color attracts butterflies, bees, and hummingbirds. Borders, perennial garden.

Butterfly Bush

PROBLEMS: Can suffer freeze damage.

NOTES: Cultivars available in several colors. *B. alternifolia* and *B. davidii* have lilac flowers. The native *B. marrubiifolia* has orange flowers. Wooly butterfly bush and peach fuzz–like foliage.

BUTTONBUSH

Cephalanthus occidentalis
(sef-ah-LAN-thus ock-sih-DEN-tal-is)

Deciduous—Sun/Part Shade
Ht. 10'–12' Spread 10'–12'
Spacing: 6'–8'

Buttonbush

HABIT: Bush or small tree with round, fragrant pale pink to white flowers that bloom all summer in the sun, off and on in the shade. Will grow in wet soil and even in shallow water.

CULTURE: Easy to grow in wet soils but adapts to normal beds. Is even drought tolerant.

USES: Attracts bees, butterflies, and waterfowl.

PROBLEMS: Few other than hard to find in the nursery trade. Chance of freeze damage in severe winters.

NOTES: Native Americans used buttonbush for a number of medicinal purposes. The root and bark were used to treat eye disorders; the bark was chewed to relieve toothaches and was boiled and used to treat headaches, dysentery, fevers, and stomachaches.

CAMELLIA

Camellia spp.
(kuh-MEEL-yuh)

Evergreen—Part Shade
Ht. 6'–8' Spread 3'–6'
Spacing 3'–5'

HABIT: Dark glossy foliage with flowers from fall to early spring. Slow-growing.

CULTURE: Needs loose, well-drained acid soil and protection from winter winds for best performance. Filtered light is best sun exposure. Full sun in the afternoon will burn foliage. Fertilize with Yum-Yum Mix, starting just after blooms fade in spring.

USES: Evergreen accent plant, border, container plant.

PROBLEMS: Scale, aphids, iron deficiency.

NOTES: Native to China and Japan. Over 5,000 varieties. *C. sasanqua* 'White Dove' is a good choice. *C. japonica* has larger leaves and flowers. Sasanquas are easier to grow than Japonicas. Japonicas have the most showy blooms. Camellias are very important plants for Houston gardens.

Camellia

CASTOR BEAN

(*Ricinus communis*) A big, interesting annual for full sun. Grows to 6'–15' with a spread of 5'–6'. Clusters of small white flowers, followed by prickly husks with shiny black seeds. Very large, tropical-looking foliage. Easy to grow in any soil; likes hot weather. Pinch off burrlike seed capsules to prevent seed from maturing. Seeds are highly poisonous. Foliage and stems are also toxic and can cause severe skin irritation.

Castor Bean

CHINESE FRINGE FLOWER

Plum Delight, Loropetalum
Loropetalum chinense
(lore-oh-PED-ah-lum chye-NEN-se)

Evergreen—Sun/Part Shade
Ht. 4'–6' Spread 4'–5'
Spacing 3'

HABIT: Evergreen or semi-evergreen rounded but open-growing shrub with bronzy foliage and dramatic shocking pink flowers in late spring.
CULTURE: Prefers moist, well-drained soils. Gets chlorotic under a chemical program. Really likes compost, organic fertilizers, and a total organic program. Can be sheared.
USES: Spring- to early-summer flowering shrub.
PROBLEMS: Chlorosis unless in healthy, organic soils.
NOTES: Is beginning to be overused.

Cleyera

CLEYERA

Ternstroemia gymnanthera
(tern-STROH-me-uh gym-NAN-tha-ruh)

Evergreen—Sun/Part Shade
Ht. 4'–10' Spread 4'–6'
Spacing 3'

HABIT: Soft, glossy foliage with reddish color, especially in the spring and fall. Insignificant flowers. Berries ripen in late summer.
CULTURE: Good drainage critical to avoid root rot. Do not box or shear this plant.
USES: Background, border, or accent plant. Can be trimmed into small ornamental tree and does well in containers.
PROBLEMS: Aphids on new growth, root rot in wet soil. Healthy if planted properly.
NOTES: Native to the Orient. Sometimes incorrectly sold as *Cleyera japonica*.

CRAPE MYRTLE, DWARF

(*Lagerstroemia indica*) Small version of the crape myrtle tree. Mature heights range from 3' to 10'. Blooms all summer in colors of red, pink, white, and lavender. White variety has yellow fall color; others have red. Should be cut to the ground each year in late winter for best bushy effect. (See "Trees" chapter.)

CROTON

(*Codiaeum variegatum*)
Tropical shrub with colorful foliage of yellow, green, and red. Use as an annual or move indoors during freezing weather.

CYPERUS
Umbrella Plant
Cyperus alternifolius
(cy-PEAR-us all-ter-ni-FOAL-ee-us)

Perennial—Sun/Fairly Heavy Shade
Ht. 4'–8' Spread 4'–8'
Spacing 2'–3'

Cyperus

HABIT: Light and graceful plant with thin upright shoots. Can die to ground in winter but returns in the spring.
CULTURE: Likes healthy planting soil best. Grows well in wet areas and even under water.
USES: Accent plant, distinctive foliage, bog or aquatic plant.
PROBLEMS: Grasshoppers and katydids.
NOTES: Fun for kids to cut stems in late winter. Remove foliage and put in water upside down—will sprout and root for planting outside the following spring. Native to Madagascar.

DURANTA
Brazilian Sky Flower
Duranta plumieri (*Duranta repens*)
(dur-AN-tuh plu-MEER-ee)

Perennial—Sun
Ht. 12'–15' Spread 6'–8'
Spacing 4'–6'

HABIT: Rapid-growing dense shrub or root-hardy perennial, with small glossy leaves and racemes of small flowers with colors that vary from light blue to purple. Bloom time is late summer to early fall. Becomes covered with small, golden ball-like drupes. Foliage is variegated. The cultivar 'Gold Edge' has intense yellow variegation and flowers.
CULTURE: Likes slightly acid soil best. Normal water requirements. Does best with organic fertilizers.
USES: Summer color, interesting specimen, attracts bees, butterflies, and birds.
PROBLEMS: Parts of the plant are poisonous if ingested. Plant has spines or sharp edges; use caution when handling.
NOTES: Interesting plant that should be used more often.

ELAEAGNUS
Silverberry
Elaeagnus macrophylla
(eel-ee-AG-nus mac-crow-FILE-uh)

Evergreen—Sun/Part Shade
Ht. 6'–8' Spread 6'–8'
Spacing 3'–4'

Elaeagnus

HABIT: Tough, gray-green plant. New growth in long shoots that arch out and down. Fragrant fall blooms hidden within the foliage. Fruit in spring is tasty and good for jellies.
CULTURE: Any soil, anywhere, fairly drought tolerant. Responds well to shearing if necessary.

Feather Duster

USES: Border, background, screen.
PROBLEMS: None, other than its pruning requirements.
NOTES: 'Ebbenji' is my favorite, since it seems to be the most compact form. *E. pungens* is the larger-growing and less desirable variety and has hidden thorns. Native to Europe, Asia, and North America.

FEATHER DUSTER

(*Diplolaena dampieri*) Small, dense shrub to 3'–5' tall and equal spread with aromatic 1½" long oblong leaves that are a dark olive green above. Underside of the leaves, stems, new leaves, and flower buds are covered with white hairs. In late winter to early spring, interesting and unique orange flowers appear. Bractlike petals and fiery 1" long orange stamens. Plant in full sun to open shade in a well-drained soil. Grows well along the coast in fairly dry conditions or with more regular water and is hardy to at least 25°F. Can be used as a small, dense screen.

Holly Fern

Wood Fern

FERN, HOLLY	Evergreen—Shade/Part Shade
Japanese Holly Fern	Ht. 2' Spread 2'–3'
Cyrtomium falcatum	Spacing 1'–2'
(sir-TOE-me-um foul-KAY-tum)	

HABIT: Low-growing, compact, evergreen clumps. Dark green fronds.
CULTURE: Likes moist, well-drained, highly organic soil in partial or full shade.
USES: Mass planting, softening element, and good in containers.
PROBLEMS: Sunburn and freeze damage are the main dangers, but they are remote. Caterpillars occasionally.
NOTES: The dark spots under the leaves (fronds) are the reproductive spores—not insects, so do not spray them. Native to Asia, South Africa, and Polynesia.

FERN, WOOD	Perennial—Shade/Part Shade
Dryopteris spp.	Ht. 18"–24" Spread 2'–3'
(dry-OP-ter-is)	Spacing 12"–18"

HABIT: Low, spreading fern. Delicate, deeply cut fronds, light green color giving good contrast with darker plants.

84

CULTURE: Needs shade or filtered light. Can grow in any soil but likes loose, well-drained beds best.

USES: Great for a softening effect in almost any garden.

PROBLEMS: None.

NOTES: Mysterious dark spots under leaves are spores, not insects. There are many ferns that do well in Houston. Do some experimenting. Other good choices for the Gulf Coast include maidenhair fern, asparagus fern, foxtail fern, Japanese painted fern, autumn fern, sword fern, leather-leaf fern, Korean rock fern, and Austrian fern. Asparagus and foxtail are not true ferns.

GARDENIA
Gardenia jasminoides
(gar-DEEN-yah jas-min-OY-deez)

Evergreen—Sun/Part Shade
Ht. 4'–6' Spread 3'–5'
Spacing 3'

Gardenia

HABIT: Glossy foliage, large white flowers in early summer.

CULTURE: Needs highly organic soil with good drainage. Even moisture is important. Adding additional compost to the beds in winter is a good idea. Greensand is an important soil amendment. Does best in full sun. Pruning, if needed, should be done fall through winter before the new spring growth begins.

USES: Screen, specimen, accent, flower fragrance, container plant.

PROBLEMS: Aphids, scale, whiteflies, chlorosis.

NOTES: A good dwarf variety exists, but it has the same problems as the full-size plant. Native to China.

GERMANDER
(*Teucrium* spp.) Small evergreen shrub with faintly aromatic foliage. Should be grown in full sun and likes to be sheared. *T. chamaedrys* is the common form with rose pink summer flowers. *T. fruticans* is bush germander with silvery gray-green foliage.

Germander

HOLLY, CHERRY BOMB (*Ilex* × 'Cherry Bomb') Beautiful, compact holly growing as large as 5'–6' with glossy smooth-edged leaves and very large red berries in winter. Does best in sun to part shade with good drainage.

Dwarf Burford Holly

HOLLY, DWARF BURFORD
Ilex cornuta 'Burfordii Nana'
(EYE-lex cor-NEW-tuh)

Evergreen—Sun/Shade
Ht. 3'–5' Spread 3'–5'
Spacing 2'–3'

HABIT: Same characteristics as Burford holly but smaller, more compact, and lower-growing.
CULTURE: Sun or shade, any soil with good drainage. Moderate water and fertilization.
USES: Medium-height border, mass, screen, or background.
PROBLEMS: Scale occasionally, chlorosis.
NOTES: 'Willowleaf', or 'Needlepoint', is a close kin with the same characteristics but narrow leaves and is an excellent plant. 'Carissa' is a compact, single-pointed, wavy-leaf holly. Regular Burford holly has the same requirements—just bigger, to 15'.

HOLLY, DWARF CHINESE
Ilex cornuta 'Rotunda'
(EYE-lex cor-NEW-tuh)

Evergreen—Sun/Shade
Ht. 18"–36" Spread 24"–36"
Spacing 18"–24"

HABIT: Low-growing, rounded, compact, very dense spiny foliage. No berries, usually.
CULTURE: Any well-drained soil, but good organic bed preparation is best. Moderate water and fertilizer needs. Best to prune in late February or early March just before the new growth.
USES: Low border, mass, or barrier. People and pets will walk through this plant only once. One of the best low-growing evergreens for commercial use.
PROBLEMS: Scale, but not serious.
NOTES: Avoid using at home if you like to work in your garden barefooted. The large Chinese holly that the dwarf was bred from is a coarse, undesirable plant. Originally from China—the dwarf forms are cultivated. 'Carissa' is a close kin.

Dwarf Yaupon Holly

HOLLY, DWARF YAUPON
Ilex vomitoria 'Nana'
(EYE-lex vom-ih-TORE-ee-uh)

Evergreen—Sun/Shade
Ht. 18"–36" Spread 24"–36"
Spacing 18"–24"

HABIT: Rounded, compact, dense foliage; small, shiny oval leaves. A very tidy plant. Flowers are insignificant, no berries.
CULTURE: Grows well in any soil, likes well-prepared beds best. Seems to tolerate fairly wet soils but prefers good drainage.
USES: Low border or mass planting.

PROBLEMS: Leaf rollers occasionally.

NOTES: This is the dwarf form of the Texas native yaupon holly tree. There is now a cultivar that has winter berries.

HOLLY, FOSTER

Ilex × *attenuata* 'Foster'
(EYE-lex ah-ten-you-AY-tuh)

Evergreen—Sun/Shade
Ht. 20' Spread 10'
Spacing 3'–10'

HABIT: Small, dark green spiny leaves, upright pyramidal growth, many small red berries in winter. Fairly slow growth.

CULTURE: Relatively easy to grow in any well-drained soil; prefers slightly acid soil but adapts well to alkaline clays.

USES: Specimen evergreen tree, border, or background plant; berry color in winter.

PROBLEMS: Leaf miners occasionally.

NOTES: Excellent plant for dark green color.

Foster Holly

HOLLY, NELLIE R. STEVENS

Ilex × 'Nellie R. Stevens'
(EYE-lex)

Evergreen—Sun/Shade
Ht. 10'–20' Spread 10'–20'
Spacing 4'–14'

HABIT: Large, dark green leaves and showy red berries in fall and winter. Spring flowers are insignificant. Extremely durable.

CULTURE: Will be more compact and healthier in full sun but can tolerate fairly heavy shade. Tolerates severe weather conditions.

USES: Screen or specimen plant. Can be trimmed into ornamental tree. Good in containers.

PROBLEMS: None. One of the most durable plants available.

NOTES: 'Nellie R. Stevens' is a cross between English holly (*I. aquifolium*) and Chinese holly (*I. cornuta*).

Oak Leaf Holly

HOLLY, OAK LEAF

(*Ilex hybrida* 'Conaf') One of the most popular of the red holly series. Evergreen holly with red berries in winter. It is columnar up to 8' in height but becomes more pyramidal with maturity. Maximum height is usually around 18'. Dense, handsome holly with a spread of about 8'.

HOLLY, WIRT L. WINN

A cultivar with dense structure and excellent foliage color. Leaves are wavy, and the red winter berries are very large. This is a superb holly that should be used to replace 'Nellie R. Stevens' in many cases.

Wirt L. Winn Holly

Horsetail Reed

HORSETAIL REED

Equisetum hyemale
(eh-kwee-SEAT-um HIM-uh-lee)

Perennial—Sun/Part Shade
Ht. 2'–4' Spread unlimited
Spacing 18"

HABIT: Slender, hollow, vertical stems. Green with black rings at each joint.
CULTURE: Grows in soil or water. Does not need good drainage.
USES: Marshy or wet areas, bog gardens, aquatic gardens. Distinctive accent.
PROBLEMS: Will spread and can become invasive.
NOTES: Prehistoric plant, very interesting and easy to use. Native to Eurasia and the Pacific Northwest. Some think it is native to Texas—it can sure be found across the state.

HYDRANGEA, FLORIST

Hydrangea macrophylla
(hi-DRAN-ja mac-crow-FILE-uh)

Deciduous—Sun/Part Shade
Ht. 3'–5' Spread 3'–5'
Spacing 3'–4'

HABIT: Big, bold-textured foliage and long-lasting blue or pink flowers through the summer. Completely bare in winter.
CULTURE: Although shade-loving, will produce more and larger flowers (actually bracts) in bright places. Likes moist, richly organic soil. Prune dead wood only. Add acidifiers for blue flowers.
USES: Summer leaf texture and flower color.
PROBLEMS: None serious. Likes a lot of water.
NOTES: Should be used in association with evergreen plants. Native to Japan and China.

Oak Leaf Hydrangea

HYDRANGEA, OAK LEAF

(*Hydrangea quercifolia*) Deciduous shrub for shade to part shade. Height 6'–7', spread 6'–8'. Good-looking, coarse-textured foliage that has excellent orange to reddish purple fall color. Showy white flowers in late spring to early summer. The bare stems are even attractive in winter. Native to Georgia, Mississippi, and Florida. Great understory plant.

JASMINE, ITALIAN

Jasminum humile
(JAS-min-num HUME-ih-lee)

Semi-evergreen—Sun
Ht. 5'–6' Spread 5'–6'
Spacing 3'–4'

HABIT: Gracefully arching shrub with green stems and small yellow flowers in early summer. Loses one-half to two-thirds of its foliage in winter.

CULTURE: Well-prepared, well-drained soil. Moderate water and fertilization needs. Little pruning needed. In fact, heavy clipping or shearing will ruin this plant.

USES: Border, hedge.

PROBLEMS: None that is common.

NOTES: Native to China. *J. nudiflorum*, a close kin, is completely deciduous.

LOQUAT

Eriobotrya japonica
(err-eh-o-BOT-tree-uh juh-PON-ih-kuh)

Evergreen—Sun/Part Shade
Ht. 10'–15' Spread 10'–15'
Spacing 8'–12'

Italian Jasmine

HABIT: Large shrub or small tree. Large, leathery gray-green leaves. Fragrant off-white flowers in fall and edible fruit in the spring.

CULTURE: Any soil with moderate water and fertilizer. Does best in well-prepared beds in areas protected from winter winds.

USES: Screen, specimen, or background plant. Lower foliage can be trimmed off to form small ornamental tree.

PROBLEMS: Fireblight (spray with 3% hydrogen peroxide in fall when plant is in bloom). Freeze damage.

Coppertone Loquat

NOTES: Native to China and Japan. Coppertone loquat is a completely different plant that looks like 'Majestic Beauty' Indian hawthorn and is a very nice landscape plant.

Loquat

MAHONIA, LEATHER LEAF

Mahonia bealei
(mah-HONE-ee-uh BEAL-ee-eye)

Evergreen—Bright Shade
Ht. 5'–7' Spread 3'–5'
Spacing 3'

HABIT: Unique shrub with vertical stems, thick spiny leaves, yellow early-spring flowers, and blue berries following. Tends to get leggy, but that gives it the dramatic character.

CULTURE: Easy to grow. Best in prepared beds in shade. Moderate water and food requirements.

Remove one-third of the canes per year if a bushier effect is desired.

USES: Accent, distinctive foliage and character, Oriental gardens.

PROBLEMS: Very few if any.

NOTES: Foliage is not soft, so avoid locations near walks and patios. Native to China. *M. gracilus* is native to Mexico and excellent for Houston and the Gulf states.

Leather Leaf Mahonia

Mock Orange

MOCK ORANGE

Philadelphus
Philadelphus spp.
(fil-ah-DEL-fus)

Deciduous—Sun/Shade
Ht. 8'–15' Spread 8'–10'
Spacing 4'–6'

HABIT: Large-growing, fountainlike deciduous shrub with dramatic fragrant white-flower display in spring or early summer, medium green foliage.
CULTURE: Normal soil and maintenance requirements. Prune immediately after blooms fade; cut oldest shoots all the way back to the ground.
USES: Background shrub, late-spring color, garden fragrance.
PROBLEMS: Cotton root rot and other fungal diseases. Messy and bare in the winter.
NOTES: Should be used more.

NANDINA

Heavenly Bamboo
Nandina domestica
(nan-DEE-nah doe-MESS-ti-kuh)

Evergreen—Sun/Shade
Ht. 12"–8' Spread 2'–6'
Spacing 2'–4'

HABIT: Vertical unbranching shoots, leggy but distinctive. Soft, delicate red-orange foliage and red berries in winter. Small white flowers in spring. Dwarf forms are problematic and are not recommended.
CULTURE: Extremely easy to grow in any soil, anywhere. Drought tolerant. Do not shear or box—ever! Can take an unbelievable amount of neglect. To lower height, cut the tallest shoots off at ground level.
USES: Specimen, container, accent, screen, hedge, Oriental gardens, mass, border.
PROBLEMS: None except that it is now on the invasive plant list.
NOTES: Native to China. We really need to stop using this plant.

Natal Plum

NATAL PLUM

Carissa macrocarpa
(ka-RISS-uh may-kroe-KAR-puh)

Evergreen—Sun/Part Shade
Ht. 4'–6' Spread 4'–6'
Spacing 2'–3'

HABIT: Very fragrant white flowers throughout the summer, followed by red plume-shaped edible fruit.
CULTURE: Easy-to-grow, salt-tolerant plant. Thick dark green leaves, spines on

branches and at the end of each twig. Thick and bushy. Dwarf variety 'Minima' grows only to 24" or so. Needs loose, healthy soil and moderate water and fertilizer.

USES: Screen or hedge, fragrance.

PROBLEMS: Few that are serious.

NOTES: *C. macrocarpa* 'Boxwood Beauty' has no thorns.

OLEANDER

Nerium oleander
(NEAR-ee-um oh-lee-AN-der)

Evergreen—Sun
Ht. 8'–12' Spread 8'–12'
Spacing 5'–8'

HABIT: Upright shrub with many ascending stems that are bare below. Long thin leaves and red, white, or pink flowers all summer long.

CULTURE: Plant in well-prepared beds with protection from the winter winds.

USES: Screen, background, summer color.

PROBLEMS: Very poisonous plant parts, freeze damage.

NOTES: Red and pink selections are the hardiest here. It needs protection in harsh winters. Native to the Mediterranean.

PALM, SABAL MINOR

Also called Blue Palm, Blue Palmetto, Dwarf Palm, Dwarf Palmetto, this is a terrific bushy palm that doesn't produce a trunk and will grow in shady spots as well as in full sun. Good to use for dramatic texture contrast.

Sabal Minor Palm

PHILODENDRON, SPLIT-LEAF

Also called Cut-leaf Philodendron (*Philodendron selloum*) Evergreen shrub from southern Brazil, 6'–12' tall, 6'–15' spread, with deeply cut green leaves up to 2' long; large aerial roots. Regular watering for optimum growth, doesn't like excess salt. Propagation from seeds, stem cuttings, and offsets. Wide, deeply cut leaves give a lush tropical effect. It grows well, moderately rapidly, with low maintenance. Grows best in a well-drained, light soil enriched with compost. Fertilize lightly monthly.

Chinese Photinia

PHOTINIA, CHINESE
Photinia serrulata
(foe-TIN-ee-uh sir-roo-LAY-tuh)

Evergreen—Sun/Part Shade
Ht. 15'–20' Spread 15'–20'
Spacing 5'–10'

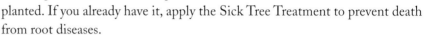

HABIT: Massive, spreading evergreen shrub. Can be trimmed into small tree. Clusters of white flowers in spring and red berries in winter.
CULTURE: Does well in any soil and has low water and food requirements.
USES: Background, screen, small garden tree.
PROBLEMS: Powdery mildew, aphids, borers, leaf spot, and fire blight, but none of these are a problem under organic program. Can be toxic.
NOTES: Native to China and Asia. Has fewer problems and is larger-growing and a far better plant than Fraser's photinia, which is too problematic to be planted. If you already have it, apply the Sick Tree Treatment to prevent death from root diseases.

Pineapple Guava

PINEAPPLE GUAVA
Feijoa, Guavasteen, Guava
Feijoa sellowiana
(feh-JO-uh sell-low-ee-AN-uh)

Evergreen—Sun
Ht. 20'–25' Spread 15'
Spacing 12'–15'

HABIT: Slow-growing shrub with thick, leathery leaves; pale gray bark; and spreading branches swollen at the nodes and white-hairy when young. Flowers in late spring are white tinged with purple on the inside. Fruit tastes like a combination of pineapple and guava or pineapple and strawberry.
CULTURE: Prefers cool winters and moderate summers. Fruit is much better in cool than in warm regions. Cold hardy, but sudden fall frosts can damage ripening fruit, and late-spring frosts can destroy blossoms. Will grow in a wide variety of soils. Fairly salt tolerant. Low water and fertilizer requirements.
USE: Hedge, screen, or windbreak. Can also be espaliered or trained as a small tree with one or more trunks.
PROBLEMS: Remarkably pest and disease resistant. It is occasionally attacked by scale or fruit flies.
NOTES: Birds eating the petals pollinate the flower. Two plants are needed to produce fruits. Native to the mountains of extreme southern Brazil, northern Argentina, western Paraguay, and Uruguay.

PITTOSPORUM
Pittosporum tobira
(pit-tos-SPOR-um toe-BY-rah)

Evergreen—Sun/Part Shade
Ht. 6'–7' Spread 5'–6'
Spacing 3'

HABIT: Soft, billowy shrub. Gray-green foliage edged in white. Although will grow much taller, can be kept trimmed to a 3' height.
CULTURE: Plant in well-prepared, well-drained beds with protection against the

winter winds. Drought tolerant and has average food needs.

USES: Foundation, mass, tall border, cut-flower foliage.

PROBLEMS: Aphids on new growth.

NOTES: A variegated form, *P. tobira* 'Variegata', exists and has basically the same characteristics. *P. tobira* 'Wheeler's Dwarf' is a compact form of this plant.

Pittosporum

PODOCARPUS
Japanese Yew, False Japanese Yew
Podocarpus macrophyllus
(po-doe-CAR-pus mac-crow-FILE-us)

Evergreen—Shade/Part Shade
Ht. 10'–15' Spread 4'–6'
Spacing 3'–4'

HABIT: Vertical-growing shrub with dark green foliage and blue berries in winter.

CULTURE: Easy to grow in well-prepared beds. Needs excellent drainage but can tolerate a wide variety of soils. Moderate fertilizer needs.

USES: Specimen, background plant, screen.

PROBLEMS: Root rot, nematodes.

NOTES: *P. sinensis* is short and bushy and very cold hardy.

Podocarpus

POMEGRANATE
Punica granatum
(PEW-ni-kuh grah-NAY-tum)

Deciduous—Sun/Part Shade
Ht. 10'–15' Spread 8'–10'
Spacing 6'–8'

HABIT: Upright growth, many stems. Showy red-orange flowers in summer and yellow fall color. Narrow, glossy leaves, bronze new growth.

CULTURE: Any soil, anywhere. Quite tolerant of Gulf Coast soils and heat. Full sun for best blooms. Drought tolerant.

USES: Specimen, barrier, summer color.

PROBLEMS: Few if any, other than not very pretty in the winter.

NOTES: Like other deciduous flowering shrubs, the pomegranate has not been used enough. Several improved cultivars exist— 'Albescens' is a white-flowering selection. Native to Europe and Asia.

QUINCE, FLOWERING
Chaenomeles japonica
(key-NOM-me-lees juh-PON-ih-kuh)

Deciduous—Sun/Part Shade
Ht. 4'–6' Spread 4'–6'
Spacing 3'–4'

HABIT: First shrub to bloom each year in late winter. Flowers are various shades of red, pink, and white.

CULTURE: Best in prepared beds but tolerates a wide range of soils. Will grow in sun or shade but blooms better in sun. Relatively drought tolerant.

USES: Spring flower display. Forced flowers indoors.

Flowering Quince

Rhododendron

Rice Paper Plant

PROBLEMS: Leaf spot, chlorosis, heat.

NOTES: I use this plant more as a source of cut flowers than as a shrub, since it looks so bad in the summer months. Native to China. Common flowering quince (*C. speciosa*) is the larger-growing variety.

RHODODENDRON

Rhododendron spp.
(row-doe-DEN-dron)

Evergreen—Shade/Part Shade
Ht. 3'–8' Spread 4'–8'
Spacing 3'–7'

HABIT: Larger and darker green leaves than azalea. Large showy flowers of red, pink, white, purple, yellow, or orange in spring. Long-lived shrub having at least 800 species. Some are tiny plants just inches tall, others grow to be trees 50'–60' tall.

CULTURE: Best in acid soil and cool, moist climates. Plant them in a 50-50 mix of compost and shredded hardwood bark or other coarse organic material. Drainage is critical. Shade, especially from afternoon sun, is important. Avoid dense, heavy shade. Feed with organic fertilizer only.

USES: Evergreen hedge, background plant, or mass. Spring flower display.

PROBLEMS: Heat, low humidity. Avoid hot, reflected-light locations. Acid-treating the irrigation water is needed in some areas.

NOTES: Fairly easy to grow in pots. Native to Asia, North America, and the East Indies.

RICE PAPER PLANT

(*Tetrapanax papyriferus*) Perennial in Houston. Large, dramatic leaves (2' in diameter) and creamy white flowers. Native to Formosa, where it was used for making paper. Spreads badly and can become extremely invasive.

SAGO PALM

Cycas revoluta
(SIGH-cus re-vo-LOO-tuh)

Evergreen—Sun/Light Shade
Ht. 10'+
Spacing: Usually used singly

HABIT: A primitive, rugged trunk, with feather-looking leaves and the appearance of a palm. It is related to conifers and ginkgo trees. Trunks are typically 1'–2' in diameter and can branch. Stems (petioles) have small protective barbs. Slow-growing.

CULTURE: Grow in beds or deep pots with quality potting soil. Need both male and female plants to produce seed. Plants can be started by seed or pups. Feed with mild application of organic fertilizer 2–3 times per season.

USE: Dramatic specimen for beds or containers and can make good bonsai plants.

PROBLEMS: Freeze damage in extremely harsh winters.

NOTES: Cycads have changed little during the last 200 million years. Native to Japan. Seeds are poisonous to dogs, so I'm told.

SPIRAEA

Bridal Wreath
Spiraea spp.
(spy-REE-uh)

Deciduous—Sun/Part Shade
Ht. 5'–7' Spread 6'–8'
Spacing 3'–5'

HABIT: Rounded overall form, many stems from the ground, showy white or coral flowers in spring. Minimal fall color. Many good species and cultivars.
CULTURE: Extremely tough plant that will grow anywhere.
USES: Specimen, accent, screen, white or coral spring flowers. Cut flowers and forced indoor plants.
PROBLEMS: None.
NOTES: Landscape snobs think spiraea is old-fashioned—I think they are missing out on a great plant. 'Vanhouttei' spiraea is a cross between two spiraeas from China. *S. bumalda* 'Anthony Waterer' has a beautiful coral flower that blooms later in the spring. Double Reeves spiraea (*S. cantoniensis* 'Lanceata') is another excellent choice. Native to Asia.

Spiraea

SUMAC, AROMATIC

Skunkbush, Fragrant Sumac
Rhus aromatica
(RUSE err-o-MA-tih-kuh)

Deciduous—Sun/Part Shade
Ht. 4'–6' Spread 5'–7'
Spacing 3'–4'

HABIT: Leaves have three leaflets that are fragrant when crushed. Plant will sucker and spread but usually not a problem. Yellow flowers in early spring, followed by red berries. Red-orange fall color. Can grow as high as 12'.
CULTURE: Grows in any soil that has good drainage, even in rock. Fibrous roots, easy to transplant.
USES: Naturalizing an area. Attracts birds.
PROBLEMS: None.
NOTES: 'Gro-Low' is a compact form. 'Green Glove' is a larger cultivar. Native from eastern United States to Texas.

SUMAC, EVERGREEN

Rhus virens
(RUSE VIE-rens)

Evergreen—Sun
Ht. 7' Spread 7'
Spacing 3'–4'

HABIT: Bushy growth. Rounded leaves do not look like other sumacs. Red berries in summer. Reddish purple fall color.
CULTURE: Drought tolerant and carefree. Overwatering is sure to kill.
USES: Specimen, mass planting, natural areas.
PROBLEMS: Few if any.
NOTES: Native to Central Texas. Deer love this plant.

Evergeen Sumac

Flameleaf Sumac

SUMAC, FLAMELEAF
Shining Sumac
Rhus copallina
(RUSE ko-pal-LINE-uh)

Deciduous—Sun
Ht. 15' Spread 15'
Spacing 5'–10'

HABIT: Small, open-growing tree. Leafy wings along stems. Brilliant red fall color. Seed clusters in winter. Spreads by suckers.
CULTURE: Easy, any soil. Can be bare-rooted and likes little water.
USES: Specimen garden tree or background mass.
PROBLEMS: None except overwatering, which is sure to kill.
NOTES: Also called shining sumac because the top of the leaf is dark green and shiny above and hairy below. Prairie flameleaf sumac is *R. lanceolata*.

SUMAC, SMOOTH
Rhus glabra
(RUSE GLAY-bruh)

Deciduous—Sun/Part Shade
Ht. 10' Spread 10'
Spacing 4'–8'

HABIT: Thick stems with foliage at ends, spreads by suckers out from the mother plant. Excellent orange to red fall color. Vertical flowers and fruit that matures by fall and remains on bare stems through the winter.
CULTURE: Unbelievably durable and widely adapt-

able. Can be transplanted easily—even bare root. Can take more water than the other sumacs.
USES: Background, mass, natural areas, fall color.
PROBLEMS: Spreads.
NOTES: 'Lancinata' is a cut-leaf cultivar that is almost fernlike. Has the reputation of being poisonous—but it isn't.

SWEET OLIVE
(*Osmanthus americanus*) American sweet olive is an evergreen shrub that reaches up to 20' in height and 10' in width. American sweet olive is the native version of the more common Asian species. Found in dry acid soils of pinelands, this shrub has an oval, open form. Rather than blooming in winter, as the Chinese sweet olive does, this native plant blooms in early spring. Small white flowers bloom on new wood and are not as heavily fragrant as the common ornamental. Best used in sun or part shade. This shrub has few problems or pests and is useful as a hedge or screen.

Sweet Olive

THRYALLIS
Galphimia glauca
(Gal-FEE-mee-uh GLA-kuh)

Evergreen—Sun
Ht. 5'–8' Spread 4'–5'
Spacing 3'

HABIT: Rounded compact shrub with small yellow flowers in summer. Texture is fine to medium. Fruit is in small though seeded capsules.
CULTURE: Needs little care after establishment. Moderate watering and fertilizing needs. Likes sandy soil or well-prepared beds.

USES: Natural hedge, backdrop, summer color.
PROBLEMS: Finding the nurseries is the current biggest problem.
NOTES: Native from Mexico to Guatemala.

TURK'S CAP
Malvaviscus arboreus
(mal-vah-VISS-kus ar-BOR-ee-us)

Deciduous Perennial—Shade/Full Sun
Ht. 5'–8' Spread 5'–8'
Spacing 3'–5'

HABIT: Red fezlike flowers in summer. Red fruit resembling rose hips in the late summer. Bushy, shrublike growth with many stems from the ground. Considered a perennial, but it looks more like a shrub.
CULTURE: Can be grown easily from seed, which can be started indoors in the winter or outdoors after the last frost. No treatment is needed.
USES: Flowers are excellent for attracting pollinators like bumblebees, hummingbirds, and butterflies. Flowers and fruit make a good herb tea. The fruit is full of pulp and seed; cooked down, it produces a good jelly or syrup. The flavor of the raw fruit resembles that of watermelon or apple. One of the best flowering plants for shady areas.
PROBLEMS: Various leaf-chewing insects like caterpillars and grasshoppers but none serious if the plant is in healthy soil.
NOTES: Deer resistant. Giant Turk's cap has large hanging flowers that never completely open.

Turk's Cap

VIBURNUM, JAPANESE
Viburnum odoratissimum
(vi-BURN-um oh-doe-ra-TISS
-eh-mum)

Evergreen—Sun/Shade
Ht. 10' Spread 5'–7'
Spacing 4'–6'

HABIT: Upright growth on thick stems. Large, glossy leaves turning a slight bronze color in fall. Bushy but can be trimmed into a tree form.
CULTURE: Well-prepared, well-drained bed, moderate water and food needs.
USES: Specimen, screen, background. Foliage is wonderful, long-lasting cut-flower material. In fact, it will easily root in water.
PROBLEMS: Few if any.

Japanese Viburnum

NOTES: This plant is often sold as *V. macrophyllum*. *V. macrocephalum* is Chinese snowball. *V. burkwoodi* is an excellent semi-evergreen. *V. caricephalum* is the fragrant viburnum. *V.* 'Blanco' is a small-leafed cultivar.

Walters Viburnum

VIBURNUM, WALTERS
Viburnum obovatum
(vi-BURN-um o-bo-VA-tum)

Evergreen—Full Sun/Part Sun
Ht. 6'–12' Spread 6'–8'
Spacing 6'–8'

HABIT: Attractive native shrub with small, leathery dark green leaves. In the spring, tiny white tubular flowers cover the plant for 2–3 weeks in February and March. Flowers are followed by clusters of blue-black berries that attract birds.

CULTURE: Can tolerate an occasional wet soil but is also drought tolerant.
USE: Works well as a topiary, espalier, hedge, or screen. Also good for attracting butterflies. Can be sheared as a hedge.
PROBLEMS: Few—this is a very tough plant.
NOTES: Compact Walter's viburnum (*V. o. densata*) grows to only 4'–6' in height. Native to the wetlands of Florida.

VIRGINIA SWEETSPIRE

Virginia Sweetspire

(*Itea virginica*) Semi-evergreen shrub for sun to part shade. Grows to 5' high and 3' wide and is found along stream edges and swamps. Upright to spreading form with multiple stems. Medium-textured leaves turn a deep wine red in autumn. Arching limbs and pendulous racemes of fragrant white flower clusters appear at the end of branches in April and May. Tolerant of many different garden conditions but likes acid, sandy soils best.

YELLOW CESTRUM
Yellow Shrub Jasmine
(*Cestrum auranticum*) Evergreen upright tropical-looking shrub to 6' in height. Showy yellow flower clusters from spring to fall, followed by fleshy white berries. Plant in full sun to look good and to attract butterflies and hummingbirds.

Yellow Cestrum

YUCCA, BEAKED
Yucca rostrata
(YUCK-uh row-STRAY-tuh)

Evergreen—Sun
Ht. 8'–15' Spread 4'–8'
Spacing 6'–8'

HABIT: Typically found growing on rocky slopes or ridges that are composed of limestone gravel. Single-trunked normally, but mature plants may branch and become multi-headed. Flowers are white and form flower stalks that rise above the plant.

CULTURE: Tolerant of the heat but also of rainfall and supplemental irrigation but very drought tolerant.

USES: Attractive and effective accent plant, can be planted either as an individual specimen or in a mass planting. Desert-type gardens.

NOTES: *Y. rigida,* or Blue Yucca, makes a good alternative. The two plants are often mistaken for one another, but Blue Yucca has thicker but fewer leaves, which are more rigid and bluer. *Y. rupicola* has twisted leaves on older foliage. Native of the Chihuahuan Desert.

YUCCA, RED

Evergreen—Sun

Red Hesperaloe

Ht. 3' Spread 3'–5'

Hesperaloe parviflora

Spacing 3'–4'

(hess-per-AH-low par-vi-FLORE-uh)

HABIT: Slender, fountainlike blue-green foliage that is fairly slow-growing. Reddish pink flowers bloom almost all summer.

CULTURE: Extremely drought tolerant; any soil as long as it is well-drained. Low food needs.

USES: Specimen, accent, summer color. Excellent plant for attracting humming-birds.

PROBLEMS: Overwatering and poor drainage will damage or kill the plant.

NOTES: The flowers are edible if you aren't spraying with toxic pesticides. Native to West Texas. Not really a yucca.

Red Yucca

YUCCA, SOFT

Evergreen—Sun

Yucca gloriosa

Ht. 3'–8' Spread 3'–4'

(YUCK-uh glor-ee-OH-suh)

Spacing 3'–4'

HABIT: Single, unbranching trunk. Spreads by offshoots to make new plants.

White flower stalk in summer.

CULTURE: Any soil as long as it is well drained.

USES: Accent or dramatic mass.

PROBLEMS: Aphids, rust, and scale if overwatered.

NOTES: Looks best at height of 24"–36". When leggy, it is best to cut off the tall part and let the baby plants take over. The flowers are edible if you aren't spraying with toxic pesticides.

EASY REFERENCE FOR SHRUBS

FOR SUN

Abelia
Agarita
Agave
Althea
American beautyberry
Bamboo
Bay
Bottlebrush
Buckthorn, Carolina
Butterfly bush
Buttonbush
Crape myrtle, dwarf
Cyperus
Duranta
Elaeagnus
Gardenia
Holly
Jasmine, Italian
Loquat
Mock orange
Natal plum
Oleander
Photinia
Pineapple guava
Pittosporum
Pomegranate
Sago palm
Spiraea
Sumac
Viburnum
Yucca

FOR SHADE

Agarita
American beautyberry
Aralia
Aspidistra
Aucuba
Azalea
Camellia
Elaeagnus
Fern, holly
Fern, wood
Holly

Hydrangea
Mahonia
Podocarpus
Rhododendron

SPRING FLOWERING

Agarita
Azalea
Camellia
Jasmine, Italian
Mahonia
Photinia
Quince, flowering
Rhododendron
Spiraea
Viburnum

SUMMER FLOWERING

Abelia
Althea
Bottlebrush
Butterfly bush
Buttonbush
Crape myrtle, dwarf
Duranta, Feather duster
Gardenia
Hydrangea
Jasmine, Italian
Oleander
Pomegranate
Turk's cap
Yucca

DO NOT PLANT

Arborvitae
Barberry, crimson
Euonymus, evergreen
Honeysuckles, imported
Junipers, northern
Ligustrum and privet
Nandina
Photinia, red tip

ARDISIA

Japanese Ardisia
Ardisia japonica
(ar-DIS-ee-uh juh-PON-ih-kuh)

Evergreen—Morning Sun/Part Shade
Ht. 6"–12" Spread 16"
Spacing 12"

HABIT: Small white flowers in clusters in fall, followed by red berries from fall through winter. Dies to the ground but usually returns in the spring.
CULTURE: Slow-growing, moisture-loving, clumping ground cover. Spreads by underground stems.
USES: Ground cover for shaded areas.
PROBLEMS: Few if any.
NOTES: Interesting ground cover that should be used more often.

BLUE POTATO VINE

Solanum crispum 'Glasnerium'
(*seaforthianum*)
(so-LAN-num KRISP-um, see-forth-ee-AY-num)

Evergreen Vine—Sun/Part Shade
Ht. 12'+ Spread 8'+
Spacing 4'–6'

Ardisia

HABIT: Often described as a "wall shrub," gets round and bushy, so it's best to prune it closer to the trellis every spring, taking care not to harm saved bits, since these may be brittle. It grows rapidly and blooms profusely after such a trim. 2" glossy dark green lance-shaped leaves, showy clusters of 1" blue star-shaped flowers spring to fall, followed by clusters of nail-polish red or yellow-orange berries late summer and fall.
CULTURE: Moist, well-drained soil, dormant in winter. Has to be annually trimmed back to the wall to retain a semblance of vining appearance. Pruning increases vigorous new growth and flower show.
USES: Colorful, interesting vine.
PROBLEMS: Few except the trimming needs.
NOTES: Plant is kin to Irish potato and deadly nightshade. Mildly toxic.

BOUGAINVILLEA

Bougainvillea spp.
(boo-gan-VIL-lee-uh)

Tropical Vine—Full Sun
Ht. unlimited
Spacing 5'–6'

HABIT: Purple, red, gold, pink, orange, and white flowers called bracts. Climbing and sprawling vine with thorny stems.
CULTURE: Must have full sun and does best in protected areas. Fertile soil not important, but good drainage is. Likes to dry out between waterings.

Bougainvillea

USES: Summer color and tropical effect.

PROBLEMS: Will freeze outside in severe weather.

NOTES: Some varieties are semi-vining. Flowering occurs only on new wood. Some varieties require the short daylight hours of winter to bloom; others prefer the long days of summer.

Fall Clematis

CLEMATIS, FALL

Clematis maximowicziana
(KLEM-uh-tiss macks-ih-moe
-vitch-ee-AY-nuh)

Perennial Vine—Sun/Shade
Ht. 12'+ Spread 12'+
Spacing 3'–6'

HABIT: Vigorous semi-evergreen high-climbing vine with profusion of fragrant 1" white flowers in the late summer.

CULTURE: Easy to grow in any well-drained soil. Low to moderate water and light fertilizer needs. Don't prune the first year.

USES: Climbing vine for fences, arbors, and decorative screens. Late-summer flower color.

PROBLEMS: Somewhat aggressive.

NOTES: Also called sweet autumn clematis. Native to Japan. *C.* × *jackmanii* also does pretty well here in filtered light. Scarlet clematis (*C. texensis*) is native and has small, unusual red flowers.

CORAL VINE

(*Antigonon leptopus*) Deciduous vine for sun to light shade that grows to 20'–30' with a spread of 10'–20'. Large-growing with dark green foliage and bright pink flowers from late summer through fall. Freezes to the ground in harsh winters but returns in the spring.

CROSSVINE
Iron Crossvine
Bignonia capreolata
(big-NONE-ee-uh kep-ree-o-LAY-tuh)

Evergreen Vine—Sun/Part Shade
Ht. 12'+ Spread 12'+
Spacing 4'–8'

HABIT: Wide-spreading vine that climbs by tendrils and has unusual yellow and red flowers in the spring. Solid red selections also available.
CULTURE: Any soil, sun or shade. Moderate water and fertilization. Easy to control, usually.
USES: Vine for fences, overhead structures, and decorative screens.
PROBLEMS: Few if any.
NOTES: Interesting vine to use because it hasn't been used much. Native to Texas and the southern United States.

Crossvine

GRAPE
Vitis spp.
(VIE-tis)

Deciduous Vine—Sun
Ht. 12'+ Spread 12'+
Spacing 8'–10'

HABIT: Fast-growing climber for trellis or overhead structure. Needs support to get started.
CULTURE: Any well-drained soil, low water and fertilization requirements.
USES: Good for quickly cooling a hot spot in summer. Grapes for eating and for wine.
PROBLEMS: Grasshoppers, caterpillars, Pierce's disease on 'Concord' and 'Thompson Seedless'. Try to buy other varieties such as Mustang and Mortensen.
NOTES: Some grapevines can get out of hand by growing so fast. Keep them out of trees. Native worldwide. The native 'Wild Mustang' is great for jams and jellies.

HONEYSUCKLE, CORAL
Lonicera sempervirens
(lo-NISS-er-uh sem-per-VYE-rens)

Evergreen Vine—Sun
Ht. 12'+ Spread 12'+
Spacing 3'–8'

HABIT: Climbing vine that needs support to start. Coral red flowers all summer.
CULTURE: Grows well in any soil. Is drought tolerant but does better with irrigation—unless overwatered.
USES: Climbing vine for fences, walls, arbors, and decorative screens.
PROBLEMS: Few if any once established.
NOTES: Good plant for attracting hummingbirds. *L. sempervirens* 'Sulphurea' is a beautiful yellow-flowering variety. Native from eastern

Coral Honeysuckle

103

United States to Texas. White Japanese honeysuckle should not be planted—it should be removed.

Horseherb

HORSEHERB
Straggler Daisy, Prostrate Lawnflower
Calyptocarpus vialis
(ka-lip-toe-CAR-pus vi-AL-iss)

Deciduous to Semi-evergreen Ground Cover—Shade/Part Shade
Ht. 8"–10" Spread 18"–36"
Spacing 12"–15"

HABIT: Terrific everblooming tiny yellow flowers. Mostly evergreen in the southern half of the state. Freezes to the ground in the northern areas but returns each spring.
CULTURE: Very easy to grow in any soil. Drought tolerant and pest free. Can be mowed.
USES: Natural ground cover. Should be used more. Looks terrific when planted with wild violets.
PROBLEMS: Some people still consider it a weed—that's too bad.
NOTES: This is the most underused plant in Texas.

Boston Ivy

IVY, BOSTON
Parthenocissus tricuspidata 'Lowii'
(par-then-oh-SIS-us try-cus-pih-DAY-tuh)

Deciduous Vine—Sun/Shade
Height and spread unlimited
Spacing 6'–8'

HABIT: Fast-growing, clinging vine. No showy flowers, but fall color that ranges from weak reddish brown to bright scarlet.
CULTURE: Easy to grow almost anywhere. Likes good bed preparation and partial shade best.
USES: Vine for brick, wood, or other slick surfaces.
PROBLEMS: Black caterpillars in spring.
NOTES: Native to China and Japan. 'Beverly Brooks' is the large-leafed plant, and 'Lowii' is the small-leafed plant that I prefer.

English Ivy

IVY, ENGLISH
Hedera helix
(HEAD-er-uh HE-lix)

Evergreen Vine/Ground Cover—Shade/Part Shade
Ht. 1'–50'
Spacing 4' (Vine), 12" (Ground cover)

HABIT: Relatively fast-growing vine for northern exposure or other shady spot. Excellent ground cover for shade or partial shade. Will climb any surface.
CULTURE: Needs good bed preparation, good drainage, and mulch for establishment. Keep trimmed from windows, eaves, and the canopy of trees.
USES: Ground cover for shade and part sun, vine for shade.
PROBLEMS: Aphids, cotton root rot, leaf spot, root and stem fungus. The diseases can be controlled with cornmeal, garlic, or hydrogen peroxide.
NOTES: Persian ivy is a much better choice than this plant. 'Needlepoint' and 'Hahns' are smaller-leafed cultivars. 'Wilsoni' is a crinkled-leaf choice. Native to Europe, Asia, and Africa.

IVY, FIG
Climbing Fig, Creeping Fig
Ficus pumila
(FIE-cus PEW-mi-luh)

Evergreen Vine—Sun/Shade
Ht. 12'+ Spread 12'+
Spacing 3'–5'

HABIT: Small-leafed climbing vine that needs no support. Climbs by aerial roots.
CULTURE: Prefers a moist, well-drained soil and high humidity. Needs protection from winter winds. Sunny southern exposure is best.
USES: Climbing vine for courtyards, conservatories, garden rooms, and walls in general.
PROBLEMS: Cosmetic freeze damage in severe winters here.
NOTES: Native to Southeast Asia and Japan.

IVY, GILL

(*Glechoma hederacea*) Also called ground ivy, a most carefree but invasive ground cover. Rounded leaves, grows in any soil in shade. Small purple flowers in spring.

IVY, PERSIAN
Hedera colchica
(HEAD-er-uh KOL-chi-kuh)

Evergreen Vine/Ground Cover—
Shade/Full Sun
Ht. 1'–50'
Spacing 12"–18"

Gill Ivy

HABIT: Beautiful ground cover that has oval to heart-shaped slightly cupped leaves, 3"–7" wide (largest leaves of all ivies). Will climb aggressively 10'–40' if allowed and can travel that far in spread.

CULTURE: Regular water and fertilizer needs. Very tough and easy to grow.
USES: Ground cover for larger areas, mostly for shade. Better-looking and less problematic than English ivy. The leaves are prettier, and it doesn't get the black spots and other diseases that plague English ivy.
PROBLEMS: Not as easy to find in nurseries as English ivy.
NOTES: One of my favorite ground covers.
Much better than English ivy. Should be used more. I hope other landscape architects will start specifying it.

JASMINE, ASIAN
Asiatic Jasmine, Japanese Star Jasmine
Trachelospermum asiaticum
(tray-kell-oh-SPER-mum ah-she-AT-ti-cum)

Evergreen Ground Cover—Sun/Shade
Ht. 6"–12"

Asian Jasmine

HABIT: Dense, low-growing ground cover that will climb but not readily. Small oval leaves, no flowers.
CULTURE: Needs moist, well-drained, well-prepared soil for establishment. Once established, fairly drought tolerant. Cut down by mowing at highest setting

in late winter—again in July if wanted. Keep the mower blades sharp.
USES: Ground cover for large areas. Will also vine slowly.
PROBLEMS: Extreme winters can severely damage or kill this plant. Average winters will often burn the foliage brown, but it recovers in spring.
NOTES: A variegated form and a dwarf called 'Elegans' now exist. They're not too impressive. Native to Japan and Korea. If your jasmine has flowers, it's Confederate or yellow star jasmine, not this plant.

Confederate Jasmine

JASMINE, CONFEDERATE
Trachelospermum jasminoides
(tray-kell-lo-SPER-mum jazz-min-OY-deez)

Evergreen Vine—Sun/Shade
Ht. 12'+ Spread 12'+
Spacing 3'–5'

HABIT: Fast-growing, open, climbing vine with dark green leaves, white flowers in summer. Will bloom in sun or shade. Requires support to climb.
CULTURE: Well-prepared, well-drained beds. Moderate water and fertilizer needs.
USES: Climbing vine for fence, trellis, pole, or decorative screen.
PROBLEMS: Very few. Can get into trees and be a little of a maintenance issue.
NOTES: Yellow jasmine (*T. mandaianum*) is lemon scented and even more cold tolerant.

Carolina Jessamine

JESSAMINE, CAROLINA
Gelsemium sempervirens
(jel-SEE-mee-um sem-per-VYE-rens)

Evergreen Vine—Sun
Ht. 12'+ Spread 12'+
Spacing 4'–8'

HABIT: Climbing vine that needs support to start. Profuse yellow flowers in the early spring. Will sometimes bloom during warm spells in winter—no problem.
CULTURE: Well-prepared soil, good drainage, moderate water and fertilizer. Top of plant sometimes needs thinning to prevent a large mass from forming. Will grow in shade but not bloom well.
USES: Climbing vine in full sun for arbors, fences, walls, screens. Early spring color. Should not be used as a ground cover.
PROBLEMS: All parts of plant are poisonous, but not to the touch. Warn the kids not to fool with the flowers.
NOTES: Is not a jasmine. Native to East Texas, Florida, and Virginia.

Silver Lacevine

LACEVINE, SILVER
Polygonum aubertii
(poe-LIG-ih-num awe-BERT-ee-eye)

Deciduous Vine—Sun
Ht. 12'+ Spread 12'+
Spacing 4'–8'

HABIT: Fast-growing, climbing vine; spreads by rhizomes. Twining character. Small white flowers in summer.
CULTURE: Easy to grow, drought tolerant, low fertilizer requirements.
USES: Climbing vine for hot, dry areas; summer flower color.
PROBLEMS: Can be aggressive and weedlike.
NOTES: Native to China.

LIRIOPE

Monkey Grass, Lilyturf
Liriope muscari
(li-RYE-oh-pee mus-KAH-ree)

Evergreen Ground Cover—Sun/Shade
Ht. 9"–15"
Spacing 12"

Liriope

HABIT: Grasslike clumps that spread by underground stems to form a solid mass planting. Has primarily one flush of growth in the spring. Blue flowers on stalks in early summer.
CULTURE: Easy to grow in well-prepared beds that drain well. Does best in shade or partial shade. Mow or clip down to 3" in late winter just before the new spring growth. Easy to divide and transplant anytime.
USES: Low border or ground cover. Good for texture change.
PROBLEMS: Snails and slugs sometimes, though usually not a big problem.
NOTES: Avoid the variegated forms. My favorites are the green forms, 'Big Blue' and 'Majestic'. The giant form, *L. gigantea*, is also good. Native to China and Japan.

MANDEVILLA

Mandevilla × 'Alice du Pont'
(man-da-VEE-yah)

Tropical Vine—Sun
Ht. 12'+ Spread 12'+
Spacing 3'–7'

HABIT: Fast-climbing vine with large oval leaves and pink trumpetlike flowers that bloom from early summer till the first hard freeze. Needs wire or structure to get started. There's also a lovely white-flowering variety.
CULTURE: Treat this tropical vine as an annual—when it freezes, throw away. Likes well-prepared soil, moisture, and regular fertilization.
USES: Climbing vine for summer color. Good in pots set by post or arbor.
PROBLEMS: Few if any. Red spider mites if in stress.
NOTES: I highly recommend for tough and dramatic annual summer color. Native to Central and South America.

Mandevilla

MINT

Mentha spp.
(MEN-tha)

Perennial—Sun/Part Shade
Ht. 1'–3' Spread unlimited
Spacing 12"–24"

HABIT: Aggressively spreading plant. Highly aromatic leaves on square stems are round, oval, or slightly pointed; smooth or wrinkly; and slightly serrated on their edges.
CULTURE: Very easy to grow. Like moist soils. Go easy on the fertilizer for best flavor. Cut and use fresh, dry and store in glass containers, or freeze and store in plastic. It's always best to use mints fresh.
USES: Used to flavor all kinds of foods, especially green peas, salads,

desserts, and drinks. Mints are best taken in teas. Ground cover in areas of wet soil.
PROBLEMS: Some chewing insects but none serious. Whiteflies and aphids occasionally. Most mints are aggressive spreaders and hard to keep under control.
NOTES: Divided into two groups according to fragrance: the spearmints, *M. spicata,* and the peppermints, *M. pipervita.*

Morning Glory

MORNING GLORY

(*Ipomoea* spp.) Easy to grow from seed, likes poor soil. Can be invasive. Moonflower (*I. alba*) has large white blossoms that open at night.

OPHIOPOGON
Mondo Grass, Dwarf Monkey Grass
Ophiopogon japonicus
(oh-fee-oh-POE-gon juh-PON-ih-kus)

Evergreen Ground Cover—Sun/Shade
Ht. 8"–10"
Spacing 9"

HABIT: Low-growing grasslike ground cover. Grows in clumps but spreads by rhizomes to form a solid mass.
CULTURE: Best in shade or partial shade but will grow in sun. Needs even moisture and regular fertilization. Mow down once a year in late winter just before the new growth breaks.
USES: Low ground cover for small- to medium-sized areas.
PROBLEMS: Nematodes, rabbits.
NOTES: A dwarf form, *O. japonicus* 'Nana', is very compact, dark green, and slow-growing. It should be planted 6" on center or closer. A black form exists that is expensive and extremely slow-growing. Native to Japan and Korea.

Passion Vine

PASSION VINE
Passiflora incarnata
(pass-sih-FLORE-uh in-kar-NAY-tuh)

Perennial Vine—Sun
Ht. 12'+ Spread 12'+
Spacing 3'–6'

HABIT: Large, deeply cut leaves. Climbs quickly by tendrils. Blooms almost all summer with spectacular flowers that are purple and white. Other color selections are available.
CULTURE: Easy to grow in any soil, drought tolerant. Dies to the ground each winter but returns in spring. Some varieties are evergreen.
USES: Summer climbing vine, flower display.
PROBLEMS: The Gulf Fritillary butterfly larvae love this plant and will do some damage. But a little damage is worth it to have this beautiful insect in the garden.
NOTES: Native from East Texas to Florida. The introduced varieties also have dramatic flowers, but most are not winter hardy. A tea made from the leaves is a relaxing drink and excellent before bedtime. Maypops are the yellow-orange pulp fruit that can be used for jellies and jams.

PURPLE HEART

Purple Wandering Jew, Purple Queen,
Lady in the Bark
Setcreasea pallida
(set-KRESS-ee-uh PA-lih-duh)

Perennial Ground Cover—
Sun/Part Shade
Ht. 12"–18" Spread 24"
Spacing 12"–18"

HABIT: White, pink, or light purple flower in spring and summer.

CULTURE: Easy to grow in well-drained soil.

USES: Pots, hanging baskets, colorful ground cover, effective annual color. Looks great when used with pink verbena.

PROBLEMS: Few if any.

NOTES: An excellent plant for dependably returning perennial color.

RANGOON VINE

Rangoon Creeper, Drunken Sailor,
Scarlet Rangoon
Quisqualis indica
(quiz-KWAL-iss IN-dih-kuh)

Tender Evergreen Vine—Sun
Ht. 30'+ Spread 30'+
Spacing 20'

Rangoon Vine

HABIT: Gorgeous, lush, root-hardy, fast-growing twining vine with very fragrant white, pink, and red flower clusters all summer and fall. Flowers open white, change to pink, then to bright red over a 2–3-day period. Fairly drought tolerant.

CULTURE: Average water and fertilizer needs. Once established, is drought tolerant. Easy to grow from seeds or transplants in the spring. Likes rich, healthy soils.

USES: Fast-growing colorful vine, attracts butterflies, adds evening garden fragrance.

PROBLEMS: Can become invasive.

NOTES: Vine that should be used more. Very dramatic.

SEDUM

(*Sedum* spp.) Evergreen succulent ground cover for sun to part shade. Growing heights vary greatly. White, pink, rose, yellow, or red flowers. Easily damaged by foot traffic or pets when the succulent leaves and stems are crushed. Native to Europe and Asia. Good for small areas, Oriental gardens, rock gardens, stone walls, and small accent areas.

109

THUNBERGIA

'Clock Vine' or 'Black-Eyed Susan Vine' (*T. alata*) Tender perennial vine from tropical Africa and Asia with showy yellow or orange flowers. Useful in hanging baskets and large pots or to cover fences. Easy to grow in full sun with afternoon shade and evenly moist, warm temperatures. Likes rich organic soil best. Can be invasive.

Thunbergia

THYME, CREEPING

Thymus spp.
(TIME-us)

Perennial Ground Cover—Sun
Ht. 1"–18"
Spacing 6"–12"

HABIT: Low-growing and spreading herb with flowers of white, pink, or lavender. Three groups: upright subshrubs 12"–18", creeping herbs 3"–6", and flat creepers 1"–2" tall. The larger plants are the culinary forms.

CULTURE: Needs well-drained, well-prepared beds. Protection from the strong afternoon sun is ideal. Moderate fertilizer and water needs.

USES: Ground cover, perennial gardens, containers and baskets, fragrance.

PROBLEMS: Extreme weather fluctuations.

NOTES: The creeping thymes cross-pollinate freely, causing a mix of flower color, but that is nice. Coconut, lemon, caraway, and mother of thyme are good landscape choices.

Trumpet Vine

TRUMPET VINE

Campsis radicans
(KAMP-sis RAD-ee-kans)

Deciduous Vine—Sun/Part Shade
Ht. 12'+ Spread 12'+
Spacing 5'–8'

HABIT: Large sprawling vine with showy orange-and-red trumpetlike flowers that bloom all summer. Climbs by aerial roots. Bare in winter.

CULTURE: Easy to grow in any soil, drought tolerant. Prune back to the main trunk after leaves fall in the spring.

USES: Climbing vine for fences, arbors, screens, or poles. Summer flower color.

PROBLEMS: Highly invasive and spreads very aggressively, causing serious maintenance problems.

NOTES: Native to the East Coast, Florida, and Texas. 'Madame Galen', introduced by French nurseries, doesn't spread as much as the native plant. *C. radicans* 'Flava' has pure yellow flowers. *C.* x 'Crimson Trumpet' is a pure red.

VINCA

Vinca major (minor)
(VIN-cuh)

Evergreen Ground Cover—
Shade/Part Shade
Ht. 6"–18"
Spacing 12"

HABIT: Coarse ground cover for large areas in shade. Spreads quickly and has blue flowers in late spring.

CULTURE: Plant in any soil in shade. Relatively drought tolerant once established.

USES: Good plant for a naturally wooded area.

PROBLEMS: Leaf rollers, cutworms. Usually looks terrible mid to late summer.

NOTES: Native to Europe and Asia. Not very good to use on residential property where closely inspected. *V. major* is the large-leafed, more commonly used variety. *V. minor* has smaller, shinier leaves, is more refined in appearance, and can tolerate more sun.

Variegated Vinca Major

VIRGINIA CREEPER

Parthenocissus quinquefolia
(par-thuh-no-SIS-us kwin-kwih-FOE-lee-uh)

Deciduous Vine/Ground Cover—
Sun/Shade
Ht. 12'+ Spread 12'+
Spacing 3'–8'

HABIT: Vigorous high-climbing vine. Looser growth and larger leaves than Boston ivy. Red foliage in fall.

CULTURE: Needs pruning to keep under control. Any soil in sun or shade. Does best in full sun. Responds well to well-prepared beds and moderate water and fertilizer.

USES: Interesting texture and good fall color. Good for arbor, fence, or large building. Makes an effective natural-looking ground cover, especially for large areas.

PROBLEMS: None serious.

NOTES: Often confused with poison ivy, but this plant has five leaflets instead of poison ivy's three. Native to Texas and eastern United States.

Virginia Creeper

WINTERCREEPER, PURPLE

Euonymus fortunei 'Coloratus'
(you-ON-eh-mus for-TUNE-ee-eye)

Evergreen Ground Cover—
Sun/Part Shade
Ht. 8"–12"
Spacing 12"

HABIT: Evergreen ground cover, spreads by runners; reddish fall color that lasts through winter.

CULTURE: Well-drained, well-prepared beds; moderate water and fertilization requirements. Sun or partial shade is best exposure. Establishes fast if planted properly with mulch applied after planting.

USES: Ground cover for large areas.

PROBLEMS: Scale occasionally.

NOTES: Avoid *E. radicans* and other larger-leafed varieties. Native to China.

WISTERIA, CHINESE
Wisteria sinensis
(wiss-TER-ee-uh sigh-NEN-sis)

Deciduous Vine—Sun/Part Shade
Ht. 12'+ Spread 12'+
Spacing 8'–10'

HABIT: Fast-growing twining vine that can grow to great heights. Purple spring flowers. 'Alba' has white flowers. Japanese wisteria (*W. floribunda*) has longer flowers that don't open until the foliage is on the plant. Wisteria climbs clockwise. Most vines climb counter-clockwise.
CULTURE: Easy to grow in any soil.
USES: Climbing vine for arbor, fence, or wall. Spring flowers.
PROBLEMS: Can take over if not pruned to keep in shape. Grasshoppers.
NOTES: Most wisteria are native to China. Many gardeners have difficulty getting wisteria to bloom.

WISTERIA, EVERGREEN
Millettia reticulata
(mill-LEE-she-uh re-ti-cue-LAY-tuh)

Evergreen Vine—Sun/Part Shade
Ht. 12'+ Spread 12'+
Spacing 5'–8'

HABIT: Climbing vine having lighter and more refined growth and texture than regular wisteria. Sparse purple orchidlike flowers in summer.
CULTURE: Loose, well-drained, highly organic soil. Moderate water and fertilizer.
USES: Evergreen climbing vine for fences, arbors, and other structures.
PROBLEMS: A few caterpillar attacks.
NOTES: Native to China.

Evergreen Wisteria

EASY REFERENCE FOR GROUND COVERS AND VINES

GROUND COVERS FOR SUN	GROUND COVERS FOR SHADE
Honeysuckle, native	Ardisia
Jasmine, Asian	Horseherb
Liriope	Ivy, Boston
Ophiopogon	Ivy, English
Purple Heart	Ivy, gill
Sedum	Ivy, Persian
Thyme, creeping	Jasmine, Asian
Vinca minor	Liriope
Wintercreeper	Ophiopogon

VINES FOR SUN

Black-eyed Susan vine
Blue potato vine
Bougainvillea
Clematis
Coral vine
Crossvine
Grape
Honeysuckle, native
Ivy, Boston
Ivy, fig
Jasmine, Confederate
Jessamine, Carolina
Lacevine, silver
Mandevilla
Morning glory
Passion vine

Rangoon creeper
Trumpet vine
Virginia creeper
Wisteria

VINES FOR SHADE

Boston ivy
Confederate jasmine
English ivy
Fig ivy

DO NOT PLANT

Honeysuckle, white
Houttuynia
Strawberry, false

Agapanthus

Ageratum

Globe Amaranth

AGAPANTHUS

Blue Lily of the Nile
Agapanthus africanus
(ag-uh-PAN-thus ah-frih-KAY-nus)

Perennial Bulb—Part Sun/Part Shade
Ht. 12"–30"
Spacing 24"

HABIT: Agapanthus forms clumps of straplike, usually curved leaves that grow from a base of fleshy, tuberous roots. Leaves are colored in several shades of green as well as variegated. Their length and width can vary considerably. Deep violet blue (sometimes white) flower clusters on long stems. Blooms from early summer until the beginning of autumn.
CULTURE: Needs moist, highly organic soils and good drainage. Does well in pots. Generous watering and regular feeding are desirable. Be careful not to let the soil get dry. Good drainage is a must—likes being watered well, but hates wet feet.
USES: Unusual flowers for summer color.
PROBLEMS: Poor drainage will rot plants.
NOTES: Native to South Africa.

AGERATUM

(*Ageratum × hybrida*) Blue- or white-flowering annual, sun or part shade, height to 15", small, round fluffy flowers in summer. 'Artist Blue' is one of the most beautiful selections I have seen.

ALYSSUM

Sweet Alyssum
Lobularia maritima
(lob-yew-LAIR-ee-uh muh-RIT-ih-muh)

Annual—Sun
Ht. 3"–4" Spread 9"–12"
Spacing 6"

HABIT: Low-growing, with small delicate flowers of white and lavender that bloom in summer.
CULTURE: Requires little care but is damaged easily by foot traffic and pets. Any soil, relatively drought tolerant. Likes cool weather.
USES: Rock gardens, pockets in stone walls, small accent areas of annual color.
PROBLEMS: Few if any.
NOTES: Native to Turkey.

AMARANTH, GLOBE

(*Gomphrena globosa*) Small-growing annual to 18" with 1" round, papery cloverlike flowers of almost any color. Plant in sun and provide positive drainage. Drought tolerant and loves the summer heat.

AMARYLLIS, HARDY

Tulip of the South, St. Joseph's Lily
Hippeastrum × *johnsonii*
(hip-ee-AS-trum jon-SOHN-ee-eye)

Perennial—Morning Sun/Part Shade
Ht. 2' Spread 2'
Spacing 2'

HABIT: Spectacular spring-flowering bulbs. Long straplike foliage that often does not appear until flowers fade away. Red funnel-shaped flowers.
CULTURE: Easy to grow in well-prepared soil, but will adapt to most all soils. Clumps can be divided and replanted in the fall or winter. Necks of the bulbs should be left just above ground level when planting.
USES: Spring color.
PROBLEMS: Finding the plant in nurseries.
NOTES: This plant will naturalize.

Hardy Amaryllis

ANGEL'S TRUMPET

Brugmansia arborea
(brug-MAN-see-uh ar-BO-ree-uh)

Deciduous—Sun/Part Shade
Ht. 5'–15' Spread 5'–6'
Spacing 6'–7'

HABIT: Shrubby perennial or small tree with large bright green leaves and large, dramatic hanging trumpet-shaped flowers in many colors. Flowers are fragrant and bloom from spring to fall. Fragrance is most noticeable in the evening.
CULTURE: Best in rich organic soils and in area protected from the wind. Normal water, but heavy fertilization for best flower production.
USES: Summer color and garden fragrance. Good in containers.
PROBLEMS: Wind damage when exposed. Will drop leaves and flowers if allowed to get dry.
NOTES: These plants are closely related to *Datura*.
Will grow in shady places but will not bloom well. 'Grimaldii' is one of the toughest and most dependable perennial varieties.

Angel's Trumpet

ASTER

Fall-Blooming Aster
Aster frikartii
(AS-ter fri-CAR-tee-eye)

Perennial—Sun
Ht. 1'–3' Spread 2'–4'
Spacing 12"–18"

HABIT: Daisylike perennial that blooms summer through fall. Light blue flowers.
CULTURE: Plant in well-prepared, well-drained beds. Moderate water and fertilization requirements. Divide established plants in spring every 3–4 years.
USES: Fall color, border, cutting gardens. Considered to be one of the best perennial flowers in the world.
PROBLEMS: Cutworms, powdery mildew. Can be overwatered easily.
NOTES: Plant in fall or early spring. The hardy blue aster is the common fall-blooming variety. Many other varieties and colors available, but *A. frikartii* is the

Aster

most showy and blooms the longest. Others mainly bloom in the fall. Two good cultivars of *A. frikartii* are 'Wonder of Staffa' and 'Mönch'.

BEGONIA

(*Begonia* spp.) Tropical native from rain forests from Mexico to China to Japan. Some like almost full sun to full shade, but most like bright light (no direct sun) with high humidity. Cane (angel wing), shrub, semperflorens, and trailing begonias do well in the ground and will winter over if heavily mulched. Rhizomatous and thick-stemmed types can grow in Houston but are subject to root rot when over-watered. Tuberous, rex, reiger, and some trailing types are not winter hardy in Houston. Rex begonias have colorful leaves and can grow indoors or out. Pinch off shoots for bushier plants and more blooms. All begonias need well-drained beds but can be grown in containers.

BLACK-EYED SUSAN

(*Thunbergia alata*) Grows quickly and easily in full sun, reaching 10'–12' and covering itself with small colorful flowers that have dark brown "eyes" or centers. This annual is available in whites, creams, yellows, and gold and is usually started from seed.

Begonia

BLUEBONNET

Lupinus texensis
(loo-PYE-nus tex-EN-sis)

Annual—Sun
Ht. 9"–12" Spread 12"–15"
Seed @ 1 lb. per 1,000 sq. ft.

HABIT: Upright to sprawling spring wildflower. Germinates from seed in fall. Leaves and stems hairy. Flowers have wonderful fragrance.
CULTURE: Sometimes hard to get going but once established is reliable each year.
USES: Wildflower.
PROBLEMS: Wet soil, high fertility, and shade are not friends of bluebonnets.

NOTES: Do not fertilize wildflowers. Nurseries are now selling 2¼" pots for planting small garden areas. Best time to plant seed is midsummer as nature does. Native to Texas.

BLUE BUTTERFLY FLOWER

(*Clerodendrum ugandense*) Evergreen glossy rich green leaves, 3"–4" long, blue and white butterfly-shaped flowers, frequent repeat bloomer. Usually root-prune back 20–30 percent after blooming spurts to maintain dense growth. Grows to 6' in height in sun or part shade.

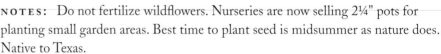

Blue Butterfly Flower

116

BULBINE

(*Bulbine frutescens*) Low-growing clumping perennial (2' height) for sunny locations. Orange and yellow or just yellow flowers in spring. Narrow foot-long aloe-like foliage that can freeze in winter. Likes sun but does well in part shade.

BUSH MORNING GLORY

(*Ipomoea fistulosa*) Shrublike perennial with pinkish violet flowers in summer. Dies to the ground in winter but returns most of the time. Will grow in dry or moist beds in the summer.

Bulbine

BUTTERFLY WEED

Asclepias tuberosa
(az-KLEP-ee-us too-ber-OH-suh)

Perennial—Sun
Ht. 18"–24" Spread 24"
Spacing 24"

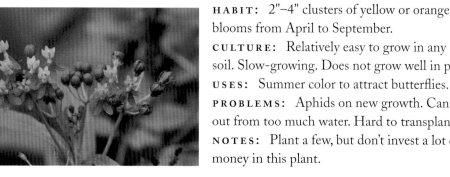

HABIT: 2"–4" clusters of yellow or orange blooms from April to September.
CULTURE: Relatively easy to grow in any soil. Slow-growing. Does not grow well in pots.
USES: Summer color to attract butterflies.
PROBLEMS: Aphids on new growth. Can die out from too much water. Hard to transplant.
NOTES: Plant a few, but don't invest a lot of money in this plant.

Bush Morning Glory

CALADIUM

Caladium × *hortulanum*
(ca-LAY-dee-um hor-too-LAN-um)

Annual—Shade/Part Shade
Ht. 24" Spread 12"–18"
Spacing 8"–12"

HABIT: Brightly colored leaves on tall stems from tubers. White varieties seem to be more sun tolerant.
CULTURE: Plant tubers in well-prepared beds after the soil temperatures have warmed in the later spring. Dies at frost. Not worth trying to save the tubers through the winter. Keep the flowers cut off. Mix rock phosphate into beds before planting.
USES: Color in ground-cover areas, containers.
PROBLEMS: Wind damage.
NOTES: The whites, such as 'Candidum' (shown in photo), 'Arron', 'White Wing', and 'Jackie Suthers', are my favorites. Mother plants are native to the river-banks of the Amazon.

CANDLETREE

(*Cassia alata*) Annual for sun. Height: 6'–8'. Spacing: 3'–4'. Open, spreading growth in summer. Yellow flowers in spiked clusters. Large compound leaves. Gets large in one season. Needs sun, loose organic soil, and moderate water and fertilization. Dramatic accent plant for late-summer color. Native to the tropics.

Caladiums

117

Canna

CANNA

Canna generalis

(CAN-uh jen-er-ALL-is)

Perennial—Sun
Ht. 2'–6' Spread 3'–6'
Spacing 18"–24"

HABIT: Coarse perennial that spreads from underground stems. Large leaves and flowers. Most popular is dwarf red. Dies to ground at frost, returns the next spring.

CULTURE: Full sun, loose soil, plenty of water, and healthy amounts of fertilizer for good blooms. Cut stems to ground after freeze. Tolerates wet feet.

USES: Use as a background flower or in large open areas.

PROBLEMS: Wind damage, coarseness.

NOTES: Easy to grow but too coarse for most residential gardens. The red-foliage selections tend to have smaller flowers but are better-looking plants. Native to the tropics.

Chenille Plant

CHENILLE PLANT

(*Acalypha hispida*) Annual foliage and flower plant; kin to copperleaf but has long red fuzzy flowers and less colorful foliage. Very tender to cold weather.

CHRYSANTHEMUM (MUM)

Chrysanthemum spp.

(kris-AN-tha-mum)

Perennial—Sun
Ht. 12"–36" Spread 18"–36"
Spacing 12"–18"

HABIT: Fall-blooming perennials, lots of colors and combinations. Attractive foliage that looks good most of the year. Some bloom in spring and fall.

CULTURE: Loose soil, good drainage, ample water, and regular fertilization. For best blooms, pinch new growth out until August 1. Stop fertilization when the buds show color. Avoid light at night, for it retards blooms.

USES: Perennial gardens, borders, pots, cutting gardens.

PROBLEMS: Watch for aphids on new growth.

NOTES: 'Ryan's Pink' is a Shasta daisy–like flower that blooms spring and fall. Foliage is evergreen and hugs the ground. Great landscape choice.

Cigar Plant

CIGAR PLANT

(*Cuphea ignea*) Long-blooming perennial. Drought tolerant once established. Tiny flaming orange flowers fade to yellow as they near the tips and are edged with black and white. Tight 12"–18" tall plants covered with flowers until first frost. A hummingbird and butterfly magnet.

COLEUS

Coleus hybrids
(COLE-ee-uhs)

Annual—Shade
Ht. 18"–24" Spread 18"–24"
Spacing 12"–18"

HABIT: Colorful leaves of red, yellow, orange, green, and all combinations. Dies at frost; very tender.
CULTURE: Needs shade, drainage, moisture, and protection from wind. Keep flowers pinched off. The sun coleus can be grown in full sun.
USES: Summer color, border, or mass. Containers or hanging baskets.
PROBLEMS: Slugs, snails, mealybugs, and aphids.
NOTES: Roots easily in water and can be grown indoors. Native to the tropics.

Coleus—'Inky Fingers'

COLUMBINE

Aquilegia spp.
(ah-kwi-LEE-ji-uh)

Perennial—Shade/Part Shade
Ht. 12"–18" Spread 12"–18"
Spacing 12"

HABIT: Delicate, woodsy-type flowers that bloom on long stems from lacy foliage. Dies to ground at frost, returns the following spring.
CULTURE: Loose, well-drained soil. Light water and fertilizer requirements.
USES: Color in shady area.
PROBLEMS: Few if any.
NOTES: *A. canadensis* is the red-and-yellow-flowered native and is very carefree. *A. chrysantha* is the pure yellow native that gets 24"–36" tall.

CONEFLOWER, PURPLE

(*Echinacea angustifolia*) Perennial summer-blooming wildflower for full sun. Grows to a height of 2'–3' with a spread of 3'–4'. Bright purple to dark pink flowers with yellow centers bloom early to midsummer. Carefree and drought tolerant. *E. purpurea* is a lower-growing variety with larger flowers. *E.* 'White Swan' is a white-flowering cultivar. Yellow coneflower is a much taller-growing and tougher perennial.

Columbine

COPPERLEAF

Copper Plant
Acalypha wilkesiana
(ack-uh-LYE-fuh wilk-see-AN-uh)

Annual—Sun
Ht. 24"–36" Spread 18"–24"
Spacing 18"

HABIT: Fast-growing tropical shrub that works like an annual for us. Flowers are insignificant. Colorful foliage all summer. Dies at frost.

Copperleaf

119

Coral Bean

CULTURE: Best in full sun in prepared beds with good drainage, ample water, and fertilizer.

USES: Background for other bedding plants. Looks especially good with white flowers.

PROBLEMS: Extensive root system often competes with other bedding plants.

NOTES: Native to the Pacific Islands.

CORAL BEAN

(*Erythrina herbacea*) Arching deciduous perennial for sun to partial shade. Grows 5'–8' high and spreads even wider. Rich red flower spikes, with 1- to 2-inch-long individual flowers. Seeds are bright red, very ornamental, and poisonous. May freeze back somewhat during winter but completely root hardy.

COREOPSIS

(*Coreopsis* spp.) Perennial that looks good most of the year and great while in bloom May to August. Will reseed and spread—which is okay. Primarily yellow flowers. Easy to grow in any soil, sun to light shade, low water and food needs. Can be planted from seed. *C. lanceolata* is a pure yellow native. Several excellent hybrids are on the market. *C. tinctoria* is an annual with a red center.

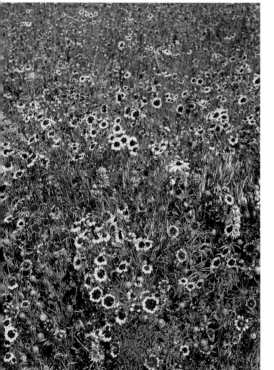

Coreopsis

COSMOS

Cosmos spp.
(KOS-mos)

Annual—Sun
Ht. 12"–18" Spread 18"–24"
Spacing 12"

HABIT: Lacy foliage and flowers on long stems. Multicolored flowers in summer.

CULTURE: Any soil, drought tolerant. Can be easily grown from seed. Plant in late spring or early summer.

USES: Summer flowers.

PROBLEMS: Few if any. Fungus if planted too early in the season.

NOTES: Plant from seed directly in beds after last frost and beyond. White varieties are also available. Native to Mexico.

CYCLAMEN

(*Cyclamen* spp.) Colorful perennials that bloom all winter. They are shade lovers and love cool to cold weather. Most species die or go dormant when weather gets hot. Native to the Mediterranean. Tubers should be planted just below the soil surface. Best in slightly alkaline soil, prefer light to medium shade when blooming and deep shade when dormant. Species will reseed themselves. Keep soil evenly moist, but overwatering will kill them.

Cyclamen

DAFFODIL
Jonquil
Narcissus spp. (narr-SIS-us)

Perennial—Sun
Ht. 9"–18" Spread 12"–18"
Spacing 6"–12"

HABIT: Bell-shaped flowers in early spring. Colors are white, yellow, orange, and combinations. Foliage of vertical blades from the ground.
CULTURE: Plant bulbs in loose organic beds with good drainage. Add a handful of rock phosphate per bulb to beds and work into the soil before planting. Foliage must be left to turn brown on the plant before removing, to form the bulbs for next year.
USES: Spring flowers, naturalized area, cutting garden.
PROBLEMS: Snails, slugs. Many selections don't return well each year.
NOTES: Flowers last about two weeks, usually less. The smaller white narcissus has same characteristics.

Daffodil

DAISY, COPPER CANYON
Tagetes lemmonii
(ta-GET-tes le-MON-ee-eye)

Perennial—Sun
Ht. 3' Spread 4'
Spacing 13"–24"

HABIT: Strongly scented leaves, daisylike yellow flowers in fall. Carefree.
CULTURE: Easy to grow in well-prepared beds. Normal to light fertilizer and water needed. Prune to the size you desire and stop shearing by midsummer.
USES: Fall color. Attracts butterflies.
PROBLEMS: Gets floppy if not sheared in summer.
NOTES: Native to Mexico.

DAISY, FOUR-NERVE
(*Hymenoxys*) or (*Tetraneuris scaposa*) Perennial for full sun. Yellow daisylike flowers spring to fall from small tufts. Very drought tolerant and prefers low-water gardens. Fall green leaves, bare stems, and foliage have strong bitter fragrance when crushed.

Four-Nerve Daisy

DAISY, GERBERA
Transvaal Daisy (*Gerbera jamesonii*) Dramatically colorful perennial that grows best in cool weather with regular feedings. Almost dormant in summer but root hardy if protected or covered. Best in rich, fertile, well-draining soil. It is a NASA-recommended plant to clean air by removing pollutants. This plant crowns at least ½" above ground, needs part or afternoon shade, must have good drainage, and blooms late winter into spring. From South Africa.

Gerbera Daisy

121

Gloriosa Daisy

DAISY, GLORIOSA
Coneflower, Black-eyed Susan
Rudbeckia hirta
(rud-BECK-ee-uh HUR-tuh)

Perennial—Sun
Ht. 18"–36" Spread 18"–24"
Spacing 12"–18"

HABIT: Fuzzy foliage and yellow flowers with dark brown centers. Blooms from June into August.
CULTURE: Grows okay in dry soil but responds favorably to moist, well-prepared beds. Needs good drainage.
USES: Summer flowers, low-water areas.
PROBLEMS: None.
NOTES: *Rudbeckia* 'Goldsturm' is an improved variety. Can be planted from seed or pots. Native to Texas.

DAISY, OXEYE
Chrysanthemum leucanthemum
(kruh-SAN-thuh-mum loo-KAN-thuh-mum)

Perennial—Sun
Ht. 12"–36" Spread 18"–36"
Spacing 12"–18"

HABIT: Large showy flowers that are great for cutting from early June to August. Returns very well each year.
CULTURE: Easy to grow in any well-drained soil. Low water and fertilizer requirements. Established plants should be divided every few years.
USES: Summer flowers, perennial gardens.
PROBLEMS: None serious.
NOTES: Cut flowers have a bad odor. This plant is similar to Shasta daisy but tougher and more drought tolerant. Dwarf Shasta daisy is also a good choice, and 'Silver Princess' is a particularly good one. Tahoka daisy (*Machaeranthera tanacetifolia*) is a Texas native that blooms all summer with blue flowers. Lazy daisy (*Aphanostephus skirrhobasis*) is a low-growing annual.

DAYLILY
Poor Man's Orchid
Hemerocallis spp.
(him-er-oh-CALL-us)

Perennial—Sun/Part Shade
Ht. 8"–36" Spread 24"–36"
Spacing 18"–24"

HABIT: Foliage resembles large-leafed grass. Many colors, shapes of blooms, and heights of plants available. Blooms from late May till September. Each bloom lasts only one day, but others follow. Blooms range in size from 2" to 8" across.
CULTURE: Easy to grow in any well-prepared, well-drained soil. Average water and heavy fertilizer needs. Divide in October or November every few years. Plant from containers year-round.
USES: Summer flowers, background or accent plant, cut flowers.

Daylily

PROBLEMS: Few serious.

NOTES: Native to Europe, China, and Japan. Daylily flower is a gourmet vegetable.

DIANTHUS

Dianthus spp.
(dye-AN-thus)

Perennial—Sun
Ht. 8"–12" Spread 12"–18"
Spacing 9"–12"

HABIT: Delicate-looking cool-weather flowers that come in a variety of colors ranging from reds and purples to pinks and whites. Some are annual, others perennial. Some varieties will bloom all winter if weather is not severe.

CULTURE: Prepared and well-drained beds in full sun. Moderate water and fertilizer. Plant in the fall or late winter.

USES: Cool-season color.

PROBLEMS: None serious.

NOTES: A good perennial variety is *D. allwoodii*. Carnations, pinks, and sweet williams are all variations of this genus. These are all edible flowers. 'First Love' dianthus blooms all year and is very durable.

Dianthus

ESPERANZA

Yellow Bells, Gold Star Esperanza
Tecoma stans (tea-COE-muh STANS)

Perennial—Sun
Ht. 8'–10' Spread 6'–8'
Spacing 3'–4'

HABIT: Showy selection of a bushy native. Blooms all summer with dramatic yellow flowers. Two varieties are commonly found: *Tecoma stans* var. *angustata* is a shrub native from Texas and New Mexico. It reaches 10' in height and has more deeply toothed, narrower leaves. *Tecoma stans* var. *stans* is a small tropical tree that reaches 25' in height and comes from Mexico and Central America. It has wider leaves.

CULTURE: Although technically a shrub, it is normally treated as a summer annual. Will perennialize in the southern half of the state, especially in an organic program.

USES: Large color plant for summer.

PROBLEMS: Will freeze to the ground in hard winters.

NOTES: The name Tecoma is from the indigenous word *tecomaxochitl*. Texas A&M has made this plant a Texas Superstar, but it's a native that has been around a long time.

Esperanza

EUPHORBIA

'Diamond Frost' Annual that produces delicate, gray-green foliage and tiny white blossoms. But don't be fooled. This plant is tough! Both heat and drought tolerant, it blooms constantly throughout the summer. Excellent alternative to baby's breath, which tends to fade quickly. Compact grower reaching a mature height of 12"–18", which makes it an ideal choice for containers or the front of a flowerbed.

Euphorbia—'Diamond Frost'

Plant in full sun to partial shade with good drainage for blooms from spring until temperatures drop below 32°F in fall. It can also be grown as a houseplant.

FIREBUSH

Mexican Firebush, Scarlet Bush (*Hamelia patens*) Colorful perennial for full sun in Houston. Grows to 4' and is covered with red-orange flowers. Prune to about 6" after first hard freeze and mulch well. Tubular flowers love the heat and attract hummingbirds.

Firebush

FIRECRACKER FERN

Fountain Plant, Coral Plant, Coral Fountain (*Russelia equisetiformis*) Free-flowering tender shrubby perennial (generally root hardy), with rushlike, hanging, almost leafless stems and bright red to orange tubular ½-inch-long flowers. Sun to partial shade, good container plant, blooms spring to fall. Easy to grow but needs humus-rich, light, moist, well-drained soil. Drought tolerant, attracts butterflies. *R. sarmentosa* 'Red Rocket Russelia', has small dark green leaves, 3'–4' arching stems, and clusters of small tubular bright red flowers. It blooms spring to fall in sun or light shade, moist well-drained soil. Hummingbirds fight for it.

GARLIC

(*Allium* spp.) I recommend that everyone grow garlic because it has so many uses. Cloves should be planted in October. Society garlic (*Tulbaghia violacea*) is the decorative perennial that has garlic chives–like foliage and pink, blue, lavender, or white flowers on stalks. Check out all the details on dirtdoctor.com.

Garlic

GAURA

(*Gaura lindheimeri*) Beautiful perennial wildflower with tall spikes and 1" pink or white summer flowers that look like butterflies. Prune to about 3" after first hard freeze.

Gaura

GAYFEATHER
Liatris spp.
(lee-AT-tris)

Perennial—Sun
Ht. 1'–2' Spread 1'–2'
Spacing 1'–2'

HABIT: Tufts of narrow stems topped by narrow plumes of fluffy purple flowers midsummer to early fall.

CULTURE: Tough, drought-tolerant wildflowers that respond fairly well to maintained gardens. Cut to the ground in winter. Can be planted from pots or seed.

USES: Perennial gardens, borders, summer flowers.

PROBLEMS: Too much water.

NOTES: Makes wonderful cut flower because the

purple color lasts indefinitely in a dry arrangement. Several good varieties exist. White varieties are also available. Native to Texas and Oklahoma.

GAZANIA

(*Gazania* hybrids) Clump-forming summer flower. Mostly yellows and oranges. Plant in full sun in any soil with good drainage. Drought tolerant and has low fertilization requirements. Grows to 12". Plant 9"–12" apart.

Gazania

GERANIUM

Pelargonium hortorum
(pell-are-GOE-nee-um hor-TORE-um)

Annual—Sun/Part Shade
Ht. 18"–24" Spread 18"–24"
Spacing 12"

Butterfly Ginger

HABIT: Upright or trailing; clusters of red, orange, pink, or white flowers.
CULTURE: Needs well-prepared beds with good drainage. Cool weather is ideal.
USES: Annual gardens, pots, hanging baskets.
PROBLEMS: Cutworms, caterpillars, summer heat.
NOTES: A little cold weather is good for them. Native to South Africa. Scented geraniums bloom only once a year and are grown mostly for their wonderfully varied fragrances. The genus *Geranium* is the true geranium. It is a smaller plant, but perennial.

GINGER, BUTTERFLY

(*Hedychium coronarium*) Easy-to-grow perennial for sun to partial shade. Height: 5'–6'. Spread: 5". Spacing: 3'. Native to Asia. Highly fragrant white flowers. It is very cold hardy. Fragrance is outstanding.

GLADIOLA, HARDY

Jacob's Ladder (*Gladiolus byzantinus*) Perennial that blooms from April to June with 18"–30" spikes with magenta flowers. Clumps increase in size each year. Not an easy plant to find. 'Albus' is a white-flowered variety. Will naturalize along the Gulf Coast. Regular glads are much harder to grow.

Gladiolas

HIBISCUS

Swamp Mallow
Hibiscus moscheutos
(hi-BIS-cus ma-SHU-tos)

Perennial—Sun/Part Shade
Ht. 5'–6' Spread 3'–6'
Spacing 2'–3'

HABIT: Upright, thick, succulent stems. Many colors and characteristics available. Blooms midsummer to fall. Large leaves from compact bushes.

Hibiscus

125

Texas Star Hibiscus

CULTURE: Easy to grow in any well-drained soil. Moderate water and fertilizer requirements.

USES: Summer flower color, specimen, pots.

PROBLEMS: Few if any.

NOTES: Native to the southern United States. There are many other hibiscuses that are wonderful plants. The tropical one (*H. rosa-sinensis*), which functions as an annual here, is the most colorful, but the hardy rose mallows—'Frisbee', 'Southern Belle', and 'Marsh'—are beautiful and perennial. Another wonderful perennial is Texas star (*H. coccineus*). *H. taiwanensis* is a durable, fast-growing fall bloomer. Confederate rose is *H. mutabilis*.

HUMMINGBIRD BUSH

Flame Acanthus (*Anisacanthus wrightii*) Small orange-flowered perennial. Tough, spreads easily, attracts hummingbirds. Is easy to grow to 4' in height in sun to part shade.

Hummingbird Bush

HYACINTH

Hyacinthus spp.
(hye-uh-SIN-thuss)

Perennial—Sun
Ht. 3"–12" Spread 3"–12"
Spacing 6"–9"

HABIT: Vertical foliage in spring, followed by dramatic flower spike of almost any color. Extremely fragrant.

CULTURE: Well-prepared, well-drained soil; moderate water and fertilizer requirements. Add rock phosphate to soil when planting.

USES: Spring color, fragrance.

PROBLEMS: Expensive for the show.

NOTES: Plant bulbs in December for early spring flowers. Plants will return but will be quite weak. Better to plant new ones again. *Muscari* is the small grape hyacinth and is much better at returning each year.

IMPATIENS

Impatiens spp.
(im-PAY-shunz)

Annual—Shade/Part Shade
Ht. 10"–24" Spread 18"–24"
Spacing 9"–12"

HABIT: Colorful low-spreading annual with tender stems, foliage, and flowers. Summer blooms of orange, white, pink, red, and purple.

CULTURE: Plant in well-prepared beds in shade after the last frost. Must have excellent drainage.

USES: Annual beds, pots, hanging baskets. One of the best flowers for shady areas, but it actually does better with some direct sun.

PROBLEMS: Cutworms, red spider mites, and slugs. All varieties are very susceptible to freezing.

NOTES: Native to India and China. New Guinea hybrid 'Sunpatiens' has showy foliage and can take much more sun with less water.

Impatiens

IOCHROMA

(*Iochroma* spp.) Shrubby tender perennial with large felty leaves and tubular flowers borne in clusters. Colors range from deep to pale violets and from purples to reds and whites. Very distinctive plant for summer color in full sun. *I. cyaneum* is the purple variety shown in the photo gallery. Related to angel trumpet but better for smaller areas. Problems include base suckers and frost. Can grow to 6'–8'. Although this plant is listed as poisonous, hummingbirds love the nectar, and not one creature or person has ever been reported poisoned by it.

IRIS

Iris spp.
(EYE-riss)

Perennial—Sun
Ht. 10"– 40" Spread 36"–48"
Spacing 6"–24"

HABIT: Vertical leaves, spreads by underground rhizomes, available in any color. Beardless and bearded are the major groups.
CULTURE: Iris culture varies greatly—some of the beardless irises (Japanese and Louisiana) can grow in or on the edge of water. Others, like Siberian, need to be continually moist. Tall bearded irises need dry beds and good drainage. When clumps get too thick, dig with turning fork, cut leaves to 6"–8", and replant, placing bearded iris rhizomes even with the soil surface and beardless 1"–2" below the surface.
USES: Spring flowers, perennial gardens, cut flowers.
PROBLEMS: None serious.
NOTES: Iris means "rainbow" in Greek, so I like to plant mixed color masses. Louisianas and spurias grow the tallest.

Iris

IRIS, BUTTERFLY

(*Moraea bicolor* or *Dietes* spp.) Native from South Africa to East Africa to Kenya. An excellent perennial iris that grows and spreads through rhizomes or corms. Leaves are fan shaped and can get 18"–25" in height. Butterfly iris will bloom from spring through summer with white flowers that have a yellow stripe down the center of the petals.

KALE, FLOWERING

(*Brassica oleracea*) Edible cabbage relative with rosy or whitish foliage color in the winter months. Plant in sun in fall; can freeze in severe winter. Flowering cabbage is also good.

Kale

Lantana

Ligularia

LANTANA

Lantana spp.
(lan-TAN-uh)

Perennial—Sun
Ht. 12"–36" Spread 24"–48"
Spacing 12"–18"

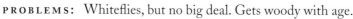

HABIT: Bushy growth all summer with flowers of yellow, white, orange, pink, blue, and purple. Trailing varieties are available. Some of the tough varieties will return each year.
CULTURE: Easy to grow in any well-drained soil; likes good bed preparation. Drought tolerant. Regular fertilization will create more blooms.
USES: Summer color, pots, hanging baskets, attracts hummingbirds.
PROBLEMS: Whiteflies, but no big deal. Gets woody with age.
NOTES: Berries are poisonous. Plant in spring. Native Texas lantana is *L. horrida*.

LIGULARIA

Leopard Plant, Ragwort (*Ligularia tussilaginea*) Herbaceous perennial for shade to part shade. Grows to 3' in height with a spread of the same. Yellow daisylike flowers in summer on long stems above large, glossy, round dramatic leaves. Likes moist soil. 'Gigantea' is the same but larger.

MARIGOLD

Tagetes spp.
(ta-JET-tes)

Annual—Sun
Ht. 1'–2' Spread 1'–2'
Spacing 9"–12"

HABIT: Fast-growing annual with lacy foliage, yellow or orange flowers. Would last from spring to frost if it weren't for the red spider.
CULTURE: Any soil, best in well-drained full-sun location. Will reseed and come up the following year but will be weaker than original plants. Can be planted midsummer for fall flowers to avoid spider mites.
USES: Summer color, cut flowers, border, mass planting. Edible flowers.
PROBLEMS: Red spider, short life.
NOTES: Native to Central America. Mexican mint marigold or sweet marigold is a herb with yellow flowers in late summer. Available in many container sizes.

MELOCHIA

Pyramid Bush, Tea Bush (*Melochia tomentosa*) This is a native 18"-24" compact, bushy plant that is a profuse bloomer, with clusters of small pink starlike flowers nonstop from spring through fall. Does best in sun with moist, well-drained soil but is also drought tolerant. Also somewhat invasive. Attracts butterflies, bees, and birds.

Melochia

Mexican Heather

MEXICAN HEATHER

False Heather (*Cuphea hyssopifolia*) Perennial for light shade to partial sun. Grows to a height of 1'–2'. Spacing: 1'. Dainty purple, pink, or white flowers all summer on lacy foliage. Very small, glossy, dark green leaves; dormant in winter. Everblooming during warm seasons. Can be aggressive and is best used as a ground cover where it has some room to grow. Attracts butterflies. Can freeze to the ground.

MEXICAN MINT MARIGOLD

Sweet Marigold
Tagetes lucida syn. *Tagetes florida*
(ta-JET-teez LOO-see-duh)

Perennial to Evergreen Herb—Full Sun/Part Shade
Ht. 18"–24" Spread 24"–36"
Spacing 12"–18"

HABIT: Yellow or golden marigold-like flowers, followed by black seeds. Upright, clumping. Flowers in late summer to early fall. Strong anise scent.
CULTURE: Likes loose, well-drained soil. Best in morning sun and afternoon shade. Very easy to grow from seed. Glossy lance-shaped leaves. Cut back to maintain compact look. Needs plenty of water and moderate fertilization.
USES: Use the foliage to season any kind of meat, poultry, fish, and eggs. Use fresh—it loses its flavor when dried. You don't need much—this herb is very strong. A substitute herb for French tarragon. Flowers and leaves are edible, but the flavor is very strong. Good for potpourri and dried arrangements.
PROBLEMS: Mealybugs and spittlebugs, which may burrow in emerging leaves during high humidity. Some spider mite damage possible during hot months.
NOTES: Mexican mint marigold is a terrible name. I don't know how it got started, but this plant has no relation to mint. Sweet marigold is probably a better name.

Mexican Oregano

MEXICAN OREGANO

(*Poliomintha longiflora*) Bushy tender evergreen shrublike herb with small, glossy aromatic leaves on woody stems and lavender to pink flowers in the spring and summer. Leaves and flowers are edible. Grows to about 3½'–4'. Sun or part shade.

MEXICAN PETUNIA

(*Ruellia* spp.) Perennial with pink to blue-purple flowers spring through summer. Grows in sun or shade. Taller types are seriously invasive. Ask me how I know. *R. brittoniana* 'Katie' is the low-growing strap-leafed variety.

Mexican Petunia

MISTFLOWER, GREGG'S

(*Eupatorium* or *Conoclinium greggii*) Lacy perennial with delicate lavender flowers from July to October. Does well in sun or light shade. Spreads by rhizomes. Should be pruned to 3" after first hard frost. Attracts butterflies.

Gregg's Mistflower

MONARDA

Nothing browses any of the monardas—not even deer. The *Monarda* genus comprises a number of fragrant herbs with especially beautiful flowers. Most are native plants, such as *M. fistulosa*, wild bergamot; *M. punctata*, spotted bee balm; and *M. citriodora*, lemon mint. *M. didyma* is the red-flowering variety. Seeds are increasingly available in mail-order catalogs, and small plants are being seen more often in retail nurseries.

Monarda

NASTURTIUM

Tropaeolum majus
(tro-PIE-oh-lum MAY-jus)

Annual Herb—Sun/Part Shade
Height and width varies with varieties
Spacing 1'–3'

HABIT: Fragrant flowers of red, brown, maroon, yellow, gold, and orange. Available in both single and double forms. Fast-growing annual flowering herb. Climbing and dwarf bush types are available.
CULTURE: Native to Mexico and Peru. Easy to grow during the cooler months.
USES: Annual beds, pots, hanging baskets. Leaves, flowers, and unripe seedpods have a delicious peppery flavor and are excellent in salads and other dishes. Source of vitamin C. All parts of the plant are edible.
PROBLEMS: Hot weather, aphids.
NOTES: Terrific plant that is easy to grow from seed.

OXBLOOD LILY

Schoolhouse Lily
Rhodophiala bifida
(roe-doe-FEE-ah-luh BIF-ih-duh)

Perennial—Full–Part Sun
Ht. 10"–12" Spread 24"–36"
Spacing 6"–8"

HABIT: Fall blooming perennial that grows well in all soils, including clay. After heavy rains in the fall, the 2" deep red funnel-shaped flowers sprout on bare stems about a foot tall. Straplike leaves emerge after blooms, then vanish in summer heat of the next season. Blooms about the same time as the red spider lily, *Lycoris*. Flowers look like small amaryllis.
CULTURE: Late-summer blooms do best in morning sun and afternoon shade. Grows well in sandy or heavy clay soils. Plant 3" deep; takes 2–3 years for a planting to become established. Increases readily as bulblets form around mother bulb. Best to dig, divide, and transplant in summer as the foliage turns yellow and dies. Flowering is triggered by late-summer, early-fall rain.

Oxblood Lily

USES: Fall color in large drifts or borders. Good to use under deciduous trees.
PROBLEMS: Finding any to buy.
NOTE: Also called Miniature Lily, Dragon Lily, Hurricane Lily. Looks good planted in front of white spider lilies (*Lycoris radiata* 'Guernsey'). Native to Argentina.

Pansies, Violas, and Johnny-Jump-ups

PANSY

Viola hybrids
(vie-OH-la)

Annual—Sun
Ht. 6"–8" Spread 8"–12"
Spacing 6"–9"

HABIT: Low-growing winter- and spring-flowering annual. Yellow, white, blue, bronze, red, purple, and combinations.
CULTURE: Well-prepared, well-drained beds, ample water and fertilizer. Crown rot, a fungal disease that chemical users battle, is not a problem with healthy organic soils. Cornmeal and garlic are the preventatives.
USES: Winter and cool-season flowers.
PROBLEMS: Aphids, cutworms, crown rot when synthetic fertilizers are used.
NOTES: Plant in October or late winter. Pansies will bloom from fall to spring. Giant flower varieties are available. Native to Europe. Flowers are edible if you are using an organic program. Violas and Johnny-jump-ups are similar but have smaller flowers.

PAVONIA, PERUVIAN

(*Pavonia peruviensis*) Shrubby evergreen to 4'. Small, dark arrow-shaped leaves and light pink flowers with red eyes. Flowers from spring to fall in full sun. Is drought tolerant and attracts butterflies well.

Peruvian Pavonia

PENSTEMON

(*Penstemon* spp.) Durable perennial that grows to about 2' in sun or part shade and blooms in spring on Gulf Coast. Penstemon (*P. tennis*) has lavender flowers. Hill Country penstemon (*P. triflorus*) is hot pink to red, and Rock penstemon (*P. bacchari folius*) is cherry red with a white throat. They also attract hummingbirds.

PENTAS

Pentas lanceolata
(PEN-tas lan-see-oh-LAY-tuh)

Annual—Sun/Part Shade
Ht. 24" Spread 18"–24"
Spacing 12"–18"

HABIT: Blooms all summer in red, white, lavender, pink, or candy stripe.
CULTURE: Easy-to-grow annual. Plant after frost danger in well-drained soil. Moderate water and fertilizer needs. Best to allow for afternoon shade.
USES: Summer annual. Great for true red color and for attracting butterflies.
PROBLEMS: None serious.
NOTES: Not widely used but should be.

Penstemon

Petunia

Phlox

Pickerel Rush

PERIWINKLE
Catharanthus roseus
(ca-tha-RAN-thus ro-SAY-us)

Annual—Full Sun
Ht. 9"–12" Spread 12"–15"
Spacing 9"–12"

HABIT: Low, compact annual for dry, extremely well-drained areas.
CULTURE: Plant in any well-drained bed in full sun after the weather turns permanently warmer.
USES: Summer color.
PROBLEMS: Too much water or planting too early in the spring is sure death for this plant.
NOTES: Always plant the dwarf varieties so they won't droop over. Native to Madagascar. Many gardeners have stopped planting periwinkles because of the disease *Phytophthora*, but it can be avoided with the organic program.

PETUNIA
Petunia × *hybrida*
(peh-TUNE-yuh HI-bri-duh)

Annual—Sun
Ht. 12"–24" Spread 18"–24"
Spacing 9"–12"

HABIT: Tender summer-flowering annual. Available in many colors.
CULTURE: Plant before last frost in well-prepared beds with good drainage. Needs high fertilization for best blooms.
USES: Summer flowers, pots, hanging baskets.
PROBLEMS: Cutworms, caterpillars, and summer heat.
NOTES: There are many heat-tolerant varieties and cultivars available. Native to South America.

PHLOX
(*Phlox* spp.) Several varieties and colors, spring and summer color, full sun or part shade. Summer, or garden, phlox is the most common. *Phlox paniculata* 'Mt. Fugi' is a lovely white selection.

PICKEREL RUSH
(*Pontederia cordata*) Bog or aquatic plant that blooms spring through fall with blue-purple flower spikes.
Attracts dragonflies and other insects. Grows to 30" tall in full sun to part shade.

PLUMBAGO
Blue Plumbago
Plumbago auriculata
(plum-BAY-go ah-rick-you-LAY-tuh)

Perennial—Sun/Part Shade
Ht. 3'–4' Spread 5'–6'
Spacing 2'–3'

HABIT: Sprawling, fast-growing perennial. Blue phloxlike flowers from spring to frost. Dies to ground in fall, returns in spring.
CULTURE: Likes well-prepared beds but is drought tolerant.
USES: Summer flowers, stone walls, natural settings.

Plumbago

PROBLEMS: Few if any.

NOTES: *P. auriculata* 'Alba' has white flowers.

PLUMERIA

Frangipani, Egg Flower, Crow Flower, Dead Man's Fingers (*Plumeria* spp.)
Gorgeous tropical with big thick stems, long pointed leaves, and fragrant flowers
in many colors all summer. Must be protected in winter. Good in pots. Sun or part
shade. This is the flower used to make Hawaiian leis; native to southern Mexico
into South America and parts of the Caribbean. Loves heat, humidity, and blazing
sun; 2–3 years from seed to flower. Easy to root from cuttings (with all mature
leaves removed) in perlite or sand kept slightly on the dry side; air-dry so no latex
is bleeding (2–3 days to dry out in shade). Prefers organic compost-enriched soil
that drains well. Houston is home to the Plumeria Society of America.

Plumeria

POPPY

Papaver spp.
(pa-PAY-ver)

Annual—Sun
Ht. 12"–48" Spread 12"–36"
Spacing 9"–15"

HABIT: Annual flower (many colors) but reseeds to return each spring. Lovely
flowers on long, slender stems. Lacy and hairy foliage. Blooms usually late April to
early May. Some varieties will perennialize.

CULTURE: Plant seeds directly in beds in September. Likes cool weather.

USES: Spring flowers.

PROBLEMS: Doesn't like the heat much.

NOTES: Oriental poppy (*P. orientale*), Iceland poppy (*P. nudicaule*), corn poppy
(*P. rhoeas*), and opium poppy (*P. somniferum*) are some of the varieties. Native to
Greece and the Orient.

Opium Poppy

PORTULACA

Portulaca grandiflora
(por-chew-LAH-cah gran-dee-
FLORE-uh)

Annual—Sun
Ht. 6" Spread 12"–18"
Spacing 9"–12"

HABIT: Low-growing annual
with succulent stems and roselike
flowers in summer. Flowers are
open in the morning and close during the heat of the day. New flowers
every day.

CULTURE: Easy to grow in any
well-drained soil. Low water and
food requirements.

USES: Colorful ground cover,
summer flowers, pots, hanging
baskets.

PROBLEMS: Flowers close in late
afternoon. Snails, slugs, and cutworms.

Purslane

Pride of Barbados

Evening Primrose

Rose, Belinda's Dream

NOTES: Purslane, a close kin, is probably better, since the flowers stay open longer during the day. Native to South America. Purslane is the common name for the wider-leafed plant.

PRIDE OF BARBADOS

(*Caesalpinia pulcherrima*) Lacy perennial with dramatic red and yellow flowers that bloom summer to fall. Yellow flowering variety is not that great. These plants love the heat. *C. gilliesii* is the shrubby tree with yellow flowers that have protruding bright red stamens. All have feathery compound leaves and attract hummingbirds.

PRIMROSE, EVENING

(*Oenothera* spp.) Sprawling perennial for sun with long-lasting showy display in the spring of white or pink flowers. Not a plant for a well-groomed garden. Grows to 12"–18". Plant from containers in the spring or seeds in the fall. Ragged looking when not in bloom. Native from Missouri to Texas. Do not fertilize wildflowers.

RAIN LILY

Zephyr Lily (*Zephyranthes* spp.) Perennial for sun to part shade. Height: 12". Spread: 12". Various colors of flowers on hollow stems in summer and fall, usually after rain or a climate change. White is the most common, but also available in yellow, pink, and rose. Bright green rushlike leaves. Plant in fall in masses for best results. Need some water but are fairly drought tolerant. Foliage looks like chives or thin liriope. Most require alternating periods of dry and moist conditions to trigger blooming. From Zephros, who was the Greek god of the west wind, and the word *anthos,* which means "flower." Hence *Zephyranthes* means "flower of the west wind." Related to amaryllis.

ROSE

Rosa spp.
(ROW-suh)

Perennial—Sun
Ht. 1'–12' Spread 2'–8'
Spacing 3'–8'

HABIT: Old roses vary from big bushes to low ground covers to large climbing vines. They are better for landscape use than the modern hybrids because they are prettier plants, more fragrant, and much easier to maintain.

Rose, Knockout

Rose, Climbing Pinkie

Rose, Ducher

Rose, Mutabilis

CULTURE: Use lots of compost, Texas greensand, lava sand, sugar, and alfalfa meal in the bed preparation. Use the same water and fertilizer program as for your other plantings.

USES: Vines, perennial color, mass, fragrance, nostalgia.

PROBLEMS: Black spot, aphids. Control with Garrett Juice.

NOTES: Many great choices available. Favorites of mine include 'Climbing Pinkie', 'Katy Road Pink', 'Belinda's Dream', Dortmund', 'Ducher', 'Mutabilis', 'Old Blush', 'Knockout', and 'Homerun'.

Rose, Homerun

ROSEMARY

Rosmarinus officinalis
(roz-mah-RINE-us oh-fis-si-NAL-lis)

Evergreen—Sun/Part Shade
Ht. 12"–48" Spread 48"
Spacing 12"–18"

HABIT: Low-growing and spreading herb. Leaves resemble thick pine needles. Light blue flowers.

CULTURE: Likes well-drained, slightly alkaline soil. Drought tolerant once established.

USES: Ground cover, summer flowers, herb for cooking.

PROBLEMS: Few.

NOTES: *R. officinalis* 'Arp' is the most cold-hardy shrub-type rosemary. 'Lockwood de Forest' and 'Prostratus' are low-growing forms. Native to the Mediterranean.

Rosemary

135

Jerusalem Sage

Russian Sage

SAGE, JERUSALEM

(*Phlomis fruticosa*) Large-growing perennial (36"–48" in height) with unusual yellow flowers from late spring through early summer. Grow in full sun and remove spent bloom spikes.

SAGE, RUSSIAN

(*Perovskia atriplicifolia*) Fine-textured silvery green lacy leaves, spiky stalks, and lavender flowers midsummer through fall. Prune to 3" after the first hard frost. Likes dry, well-drained beds.

SALVIA, GREGG

Autumn Sage
Salvia greggii
(SAL-vee-uh GREG-ee-eye)

Perennial—Sun
Ht. 2'–3' Spread 3'–4'
Spacing 2'

HABIT: Shrubby perennial with red, pink, salmon, or white blooms all summer long.

CULTURE: Any well-drained soil, extremely drought tolerant.

USES: Spring, summer, and fall color; perennial gardens.

PROBLEMS: None.

NOTES: Native to Texas. Annual salvia (*S. splendens*) likes plenty of water and fertilizer. Scarlet sage (*S. coccinea*) is a native perennial that grows 1'–2' high and looks like the annual salvia. *S. regla*, mountain sage, blooms in the fall. *S. guaranitica*, anise sage, has intense blue flowers, grows 3'–4' high, but is not quite as winter hardy as *S. greggii*. *S. leucantha*, Mexican bush salvia, is a large-growing perennial with beautiful foliage and purple flowers in late summer. The flowers are edible if you are using an organic program. *S. divinorum* is the dangerous hallucinogenic drug that should be avoided.

SALVIA, MEALY BLUE

Blue Sage
Salvia farinacea
(SAL-vee-uh far-eh-NAY-see-uh)

Perennial—Sun/Part Shade
Ht. 2'–3' Spread 2'–3'
Spacing 1'–2'

HABIT: Gray-green foliage and long blue flowers on vertical stems.

CULTURE: Easy to grow in any well-drained soil; drought tolerant, low fertilizer requirements. Plant in fall or spring.

USES: Summer flowers, perennial garden, blue color.

PROBLEMS: None.

Mealy Blue Sage

136

NOTES: Native to Central and West Texas and New Mexico. A compact cultivar is now available. 'Indigo Spires' is another tough blue-flowering salvia. The flowers are edible if you are using an organic program. *S. madrensis* is the dramatic big yellow sage.

SHRIMP PLANT

(*Justicia brandegeana*) Terra cotta to lemon-yellow bracts with small white flowers that arch to the side. Full sun. Close kin is lollipop plant (*Pachystachys lutea*), which has bright yellow bracts that are vertical. Needs partial shade. Both are used as annuals here.

Shrimp Plant

SKULLCAP, PINK

Scutellaria suffrutescens
(skoo-tul-AIR-ee-uh suff-roo-TESS-enz)

Semi-evergreen Perennial—Sun
Ht. 6"–12" Spread 8"–12"
Spacing 12"

HABIT: Tiny foliage and loaded with tiny snapdragon-like pink flowers from spring to fall.
CULTURE: Likes well-prepared beds, needs excellent drainage. Drought tolerant. Responds well to occasional shearing, which prevents thinning in the center of the plant.
USES: Summer color, border, attracts butterflies, rock gardens, xeric gardens, containers.
PROBLEMS: Overwatering.
NOTES: An excellent flower choice for your garden.

Pink Skullcap

SNAPDRAGON

Antirrhinum spp.
(an-tee-REE-num)

Annual—Sun/Part Shade
Ht. 12"–24" Spread 9"–12"
Spacing 9"–12"

HABIT: Upright flower spikes available in many colors.
CULTURE: Plant in sun or partial shade. Likes healthy soil, moderate water, and regular fertilization, as well as cool weather. Plant in late winter or early spring.
USES: Cool-season color, cut flowers.

PROBLEMS: Rust, cutworms.
NOTES: Native to the Mediterranean.

SPIDER LILY   Perennial—Sun/Part Shade
Lycoris spp.   Ht. 15"-24" Spread 6"-12"
(li-KO-ris)   Spacing 6"-12"

HABIT: Clusters of purple, red, pink, white, or yellow summer flowers.
CULTURE: Plant bulbs from spring through late summer. May not bloom the first fall. Narrow leaves appear in spring but die down before the plant blooms.
USES: Perennial summer color.
PROBLEMS: Cutworms, loopers, and other caterpillars.
NOTES: *L. radiata* is the red spider lily. *L. squamigera* is the trumpet-shaped pink belladonna lily that blooms in late summer to early fall. *L. africana* is bright yellow. *L.* × *albiflora* is the white fall spider lily.

SPIDER LILY, WHITE

(*Hymenocallis liriosme*) Perennial bulb that likes wet soil and blooms in spring. Red spider lily (*Lycoris radiata*) has red flowers in mid- to late summer. Sun to part shade.

Spider Lily

White Spider Lily

STRAWBERRY BUSH

(*Euonymus americana*)
Deciduous shrub for sun to partial shade. Bright green smooth oval leaves turn brilliant fall colors (red, orange, and yellow) reliably.
May–June flowers are greenish purple and inconspicuous. Fruits in fall–winter: red 1-inch capsules that split open, revealing 4–5 reddish seeds. Grows to a height of 3'. Native to many woodland areas along the Gulf Coast region.

THRIFT   Perennial—Sun
Moss Phlox   Ht. 6"–8" Spread 10"–12"
Phlox subulata   Spacing 10"–12"
(FLOCKS sub-you-LAY-tuh)

HABIT: Low-growing and spreading perennial that acts like an evergreen in mild winters. Blooms in spring in pink, blue, or white. Hot pink is the most common color.
CULTURE: Easy to grow in any well-drained soil, with moderate water and fertilizer needs.
USES: Dwarf border, spring color, stone walls.
PROBLEMS: None.
NOTES: Reliable to bloom year after year. Plant in fall or spring. Native to North America. 'Blue Emerald' is the best; its foliage is lush and dark green all summer.

Thrift

VERBENA
Verbena spp.
(ver-BEAN-uh)

Perennial—Sun
Ht. 9"–12" Spread 12"–18"
Spacing 9"–12"

HABIT: Low, spreading perennial that blooms in red, white, salmon, and purple all summer.
CULTURE: Easy to grow in well-drained beds, low water and fertilization requirements.
USES: Summer color.
PROBLEMS: Red spider mites occasionally.
NOTES: The natives are prairie verbena (*V. bipinnatifida*) and moss verbena (*V. tenuisecta*). The cultivated varieties are good as well. 'Pink Parfait' is a beautiful, large-flowered evergreen.

Verbena

VERBENA, ALMOND
Sweet Almond Verbena (*Aloysia virgata*) A sweetly fragrant perennial or deciduous shrub with spikes of white blooms summer to fall. Prune in early spring and between bloom cycles for denser growth. Plant in full sun to part shade. Grows to 10'. Looks like butterfly bush (*Buddleia*).

YARROW
Achillea spp.
(ah-KILL-ee-uh)

Perennial—Sun
Ht. 2' Spread 2'
Spacing 1'–2'

HABIT: Upright lacy foliage, flat-topped clusters of flowers. Colors include white, rose, pink, yellow, and red.
CULTURE: Easy to grow in any well-drained soil. Plant in spring or fall.
USES: Perennial border, cut flowers.
PROBLEMS: Some varieties grow tall and need to be staked. Can be invasive.
NOTES: Native to Europe. *A. millefolium* is a white-blooming, very tough species.

Almond Verbena

WINECUP
(*Callirhoe involucrata*) Perennial wildflower that is excellent for filling in between plants. 2" poppylike wine-red flowers bloom in sun to part shade from spring to early summer. Cut back to rosettes in winter for neater appearance. Needs part shade and well-drained soil for best results. Attracts butterflies.

Yarrow

Zinnia

ZINNIA

Zinnia spp.
(ZEN-ee-uh)

Annual—Sun
Ht. 8"–36" Spread 12"–24"
Spacing 12"

HABIT: Open, upright growth. Flowers of all colors and sizes on long stems in summer.

CULTURE: Any loose soil, fairly drought tolerant. Add rock phosphate for more blooms. Plant from seeds or pots in spring.

USES: Summer color, cut flowers.

PROBLEMS: Mildew, cutworms, red spider mites. Gets ragged toward the end of summer.

NOTES: Native to Mexico and Central America.

EASY REFERENCE FOR ANNUALS AND PERENNIALS

FALL COLOR

Aster
Calendula
Candletree
Chrysanthemum
Daisy, Copper Canyon
Marigold
Salvia
Geranium
Iris
Nasturtium
Petunia
Phlox
Poppy
Rose
Snapdragon
Thrift
Yarrow

WINTER COLOR

Calendula
Cyclamen
Daisy, Gerbera
Dianthus
Kale
Pansy
Snapdragon

SPRING COLOR

Alyssum
Aster
Bluebonnet
Coreopsis
Daffodil
Daisy
Daylily
Dianthus

SUMMER COLOR (SUN)

Agapanthus
Ageratum
Alyssum
Amaranth, globe
Amaryllis
Angel's trumpet
Begonia
Black-eyed Susan
Blue butterfly flower
Bulbine
Butterfly weed
Canna
Chenille plant
Cigar plant
Coneflower, purple
Copperleaf
Coral bean

Coreopsis
Cosmos
Daisy
Daylily
Esperanza
Euphorbia—'Diamond Frost'
Firebush
Firecracker fern
Gaura
Gayfeather
Hibiscus
Hummingbird bush
Iochroma
Lantana
Marigold
Mexican heather
Mexican oregano
Mexican petunia
Pentas
Periwinkle
Phlox
Plumbago
Plumeria
Portulaca
Pride of Barbados

Primrose, evening
Rain lily
Rose
Rosemary
Sage, Jerusalem
Sage, Russian
Salvia
Shrimp plant
Spider lily
Verbena
Yarrow
Zinnia

SUMMER COLOR (SHADE)

Begonia
Caladium
Coleus
Columbine
Geranium
Impatiens
Lingularia
Lobelia
Plumeria

GRASSES

Common Bermudagrass

BERMUDAGRASS, COMMON
Cynodon dactylon
(SIN-no-don DAC-ti-lon)

Warm Season—Sun
Mowing Ht. 1½"–2"
Seed @ 2 lbs./1,000 sq. ft.

HABIT: Narrow leaf blade; spread by stolons and rhizomes. Brown in winter.
CULTURE: Low-maintenance, aggressive grass. Grows in any soil. Does much better with ample water and food but is quite drought tolerant. Does not develop thatch, especially when maintained with an organic program.
USES: Lawn grass, playing fields.
PROBLEMS: Some insects and diseases but none serious.
NOTES: Mixing with St. Augustine and some weeds looks okay. Native to warm regions around the world.

Tif Bermudagrass

BERMUDAGRASS, TIF
Tifgrass, Tif
Cynodon dactylon cultivars
(SIN-no-don DAC-ti-lon)

Warm Season—Sun
Mowing Ht. ½"–¾"
Stolons @ 10–15 bushels/1,000 sq. ft.

HABIT: Hybrid forms of common Bermudagrass. Narrower leaf blade and finer overall texture. Tifdwarf is the finest-textured, Tifgreen 328 is slightly larger, and Tifway 419 is the largest and the best of the hybrids for residential use.
CULTURE: Higher maintenance than common Bermudagrass, since weeds and imperfections are much more visible.
USES: Refined lawns and putting greens. Also golf course tees and fairways. These grasses are sterile (no seeds) and must be planted solid or from stolons.
PROBLEMS: Some insects and diseases but none serious. Weeds show up badly.
NOTES: Too much work for home lawns. Native to laboratory.

Tall Fescue

FESCUE, TALL
Festuca arundinacea
(fess-TOO-cuh ah-run-dih-NAY-shee-uh)

Cool Season—Sun/Shade
Mowing Ht. 2"–4"
Seed @ 8–10 lbs./1,000 sq. ft.

HABIT: Bunch-type grass that is planted as a winter overseeding or used in shady lawn areas. A permanent grass.
CULTURE: Needs fertile, well-drained soil and should be planted in the fall (Sept.–Nov.) for best results.
USES: Lawn grass in shade, overseeding.
PROBLEMS: Have to mow all winter, looks somewhat artificial in Texas.
NOTES: Best of the permanent winter grasses for home use. Native to Europe.

FOUNTAIN GRASS

Pennisetum spp. or *Miscanthus* spp.
(pen-eh-SEE-tum) (miss-CAN-thus)

Perennial—Sun
Ht. 3'–4' Spread 3'–4'
Spacing 3'–4'

HABIT: Showy ornamental grass, slender leaves and flower plumes from July to October.

CULTURE: Easy to grow in most any soil in sun to light shade. Moderate water and fertilizer requirements.

USES: Specimen, medium-height border, summer flowers.

PROBLEMS: None.

NOTES: Several similar varieties available with different heights and flower colors. There are many terrific ornamental grasses that are well adapted and grow well here, such as Hamlen dwarf, zebra grass, and coastal and purple fountain grass.

INLAND SEAOATS

Wild Oats
Chasmanthium latifolium
(chas-MAN-thee-um lah-the-FOLE-ee-um)

Perennial—Shade/Part Shade
Ht. 2'–4' Spread unlimited
Spacing 2'–3'

HABIT: Looks like dwarf bamboo. Insignificant flowers, followed by very decorative seed heads that turn golden ivory in fall and last into January.

CULTURE: Easy to grow in any soil in shady areas but can tolerate some direct sun. In large areas, sow @ 2 lbs. seed per 1,000 sq. ft. Will grow in deep sugar sand or black clay. Reseeds readily. Cutting the seed heads off before they mature helps to prevent spreading.

USES: Great plant for erosion control in the shade. Can also adapt to sunny spots.

PROBLEMS: Spreads aggressively by seed and rhizomes, so be careful where you plant it.

NOTES: Stems with dry seed heads can be cut for long-lasting dry flower arrangements.

Fountain Grass

Inland Seaoats

MUHLY, GULF COAST

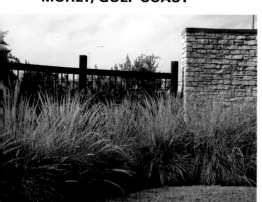

(*Muhlenbergia capillaris*) Height: 3'–4'. Native to East and Southeast Texas. Clouds of pink flowers in October. Prefers good drainage and average water. Big Muhly or Lindheimer (*M. lindheimeri*): Height 4–6'. Native to Central Texas. Silvery plumes in October. It's an elegant substitute for invasive pampas grass and has softer leaves that will not scratch. Seep Muhly (*M. reverchonii*): Short clump grass. Native to Central and North Central Texas. Light pink to cream-colored, delicate, airy flower heads emerge in October. Grows in well-drained, moist to moderate soils, as well as in moist rocky sites.

Pampas Grass

Paspalum

PAMPAS GRASS

Cortaderia selloana
(core-ta-DER-ee-uh sell-oh-AN-uh)

Perennial—Sun
Ht. 8' Spread 8'
Spacing 8'–10'

HABIT: Fountainlike clump grass with long, slender sharp-edged blades of foliage. White flower plumes in late summer last quite long into the winter. Foliage turns brown in harsh winter and should be cut back.
CULTURE: Very easy to grow in any soil. Low water and food requirements. Needs good drainage, like most plants.
USES: Accent plant; border for roads, drives, or parks. Good for distant viewing.
PROBLEMS: Few if any. Some consider the coarseness a negative.
NOTES: White plumes are good for interior arrangements. Female plants have the showiest plumes. Native to South America.

PASPALUM

Paspalum vaginatum
(pas-PAL-lum vag-ah-NAH-tum)
SeaIsle 1

Warm-season Turfgrass—Sun
Mowing Ht. ⅛"–2"
Solid sod or Sprigs

HABIT: Rich dark green warm-season, medium-textured grass that grows in a wide range of soils but does best in sandy soils. It has excellent resistance to drought and wear and is very salt tolerant.
CULTURE: Can tolerate most alternate water sources, such as waste water, effluent, ocean water, gray water, and brackish water. Requires low levels of fertilization, irrigation, and pest management.
USES: Excellent choice for fairways, tees, roughs, commercial landscaping, athletic fields, and reclamation projects.
PROBLEMS: Homeowners can use but will need to mow more often and be aware of possible fungal problems.
NOTES: SeaIsle 2000 has a blue-green cast and can be mowed even lower (⅛"). This is the grass used on the field at the Astros' ballpark. I can't remember the corporate sponsor name.

PASPALUM, SEASHORE

Paspalum vaginatum

Warm-season Turfgrass—Sun
Ht. ⅜"–2"
Solid sod or Sprigs

HABIT: In the United States, seashore paspalum is found along coastal regions from Texas to Florida and North Carolina southward. Along the Texas coast this species is often the only grass found growing around brackish ponds and estuaries.
CULTURE: Tolerant of saline soils. Tolerates brackish sites much better than Bermudagrass. Perhaps the most extensive planting in Texas is on the King's Crossing golf course in Corpus Christi. The entire golf course, except for the putting greens, was sprigged with seashore paspalum. Has to be mowed every 3–4 days to prevent seed. Fertilizer requirements are less than for Bermudagrass. It tolerates wet conditions much better than Bermudagrass.
USE: Salty sites, golf courses.

NOTES: Its adaptation is said to be similar to centipede grass. Native to tropical and subtropical regions of North and South America.

ST. AUGUSTINEGRASS

Stenotaphrum secundatum
(sten-no-TAY-frum seh-coon-DAY-tum)

Sun/Part Shade—Warm Season
Mowing Ht. 2"–4"
Solid sod

HABIT: Wide-bladed grass, spreads by stolons, most shade tolerant of our warm-season grasses. 'Raleigh' is a hybrid resistant to St. Augustine decline (SAD), and is more cold hardy than hybrids 'Seville' and 'Floratam'.
CULTURE: Any well-drained soil that is fairly fertile. Not as tough as Bermuda-grass.
USES: Lawn grass, shade.
PROBLEMS: Chinch bugs, grubworms, diseases.
NOTES: Native to Africa and the Gulf Coast.

ZOYSIAGRASS

Zoysia japonica
(ZOY-sha juh-PON-ih-kuh)

Warm-season Turfgrass—Sun/Light Shade
Mowing Ht. 2"–3"
Solid sod only

Zoysia

HABIT: Thick, succulent-looking grass. Very slow to spread.
CULTURE: Plant solid sod only, too slow-growing for any other planting techniques.
USES: Lawn grass, small areas, Oriental gardens.
PROBLEMS: Slow, but that gives it its maintenance advantages.
NOTES: Avoid using in high-traffic areas. 'Meyer' is wider-leafed and better than 'Emerald'. Zoysia can be mowed less often than Bermudagrass and St. Augustine-grass, and it requires far less edging. There are many new versions on the market. Native to Japan.

145

RECOMMENDED GRASSES

FOR SUN

Bermudagrass
Bermudagrass, Tif
St. Augustinegrass
Zoysiagrass

FOR SHADE

Fescue
St. Augustinegrass

Dirt Doctor's *DIRT* newsletter, a monthly online publication available through DirtDoctor.com.

The Garden-Ville Method: Lessons in Nature is written by my mentor and the king of compost, Malcolm Beck, one of the most knowledgeable people on organics in the country. 3rd ed. San Antonio, TX: Garden-Ville, Inc., 1998.

Habitat Gardening for Houston and Southwest Texas by Mark Bowen with Mary Bowen. Very helpful book on natural design, plants, and wildlife. Houston: River Bend Publishing Company, 1998.

Herbs for Texas: A Study of the Landscape, Culinary, and Medicinal Uses and Benefits of the Herbs That Can Be Grown in Texas by Howard Garrett with Odena Brannam. A complete guide for the trees, shrubs, annuals, and perennials that have a use other than looking pretty. Austin: University of Texas Press, 2001.

Howard Garrett's Plants for Texas. Descriptions and photographs of over 500 plants, with instructions for growing them. Austin: University of Texas Press, 1996.

J. Howard Garrett's Organic Manual. Easy-to-follow, money-saving advice on the proper selection, installation, and maintenance of organic landscaping and gardening. 2nd ed. Arlington, TX: Summit Publishing Group, 2000.

Naturalistic Landscaping for the Gulf Coast by Mark Bowen. Book contains landscape design tips, landscape installation instructions, and organic pest remedies. Houston: River Bend Publishing, 2004.

The Secret Life of Compost: A "How-to" & "Why" Guide to Composting by Malcolm Beck is simply the best book in the world on the topic of composting. Metairie, LA: Acres U.S.A., 1997.

Silent Spring by Rachel Carson. If you don't convert to organics after reading this classic, you never will. Boston: Houghton Mifflin; Cambridge, MA: Riverside Press, 1962.

Texas Bug Book: The Good, the Bad, and the Ugly, coauthored by C. Malcolm Beck and John Howard Garrett, covers the protection and use of beneficial insects and gives detailed information on how to organically or biologically control troublesome insects. Austin: University of Texas Press, 1999.

Texas Gardening the Natural Way: The Complete Handbook. A compilation of all Howard's previous books. Austin: University of Texas Press, 2004.

Texas Organic Vegetable Gardening: The Total Guide to Growing Vegetables, Fruits, Herbs, and Other Edible Plants the Natural Way by J. Howard Garrett and C. Malcolm Beck. Organic information specifically for Texas, including plant varieties, planting instructions, and maintenance techniques. Houston, TX: Gulf Publishing, 1998.

Texas Organic Vegetables and Edible Landscaping, coauthored by C. Malcolm Beck and John Howard Garrett. Information about food crops for Texas, including vegetables, fruits, nuts, and herbs. Houston, TX: Gulf Publishing Company.

Texas Wildflowers: A Field Guide, by Campbell and Lynn Loughmiller, is a beautiful guide to more than 300 species of Texas wildflowers. Rev. ed., updated. Austin: University of Texas Press, 2006.

Year Round Vegetables, Fruits, and Flowers from Metro Houston: A Natural Organic Approach Using Ecology by Bob Randall, Ph.D., Executive Director, Urban Harvest—a community garden and orchard program for Greater Houston. Houston, TX: Year Round Gardening Press, 1999.

FOR MORE INFORMATION:

Dallas Morning News column "The Natural Way," Friday, House and Garden Section

Howard Garrett mailing address: P.O. Box 140650, Dallas, TX 75214
Web site: www.dirtdoctor.com
E-mail: info@dirtdoctor.com
Newsletter info at www.dirtdoctor.com

INDEX

A

A&M Research Station, 6
Abelia, 75
Abelia grandiflora, 75
Acacia, 40
Acalypha hispida, 118
Acalypha wilkesiana, 119
Acer barbatum, 58
Acer buergerianum, 58
Acer leucoderme, 56
Acer rubrum, 57
Achillea spp., 139
Aeration, 19
Aesculus glabra, 43
Agapanthus, 114
Agapanthus africanus, 114
Agarita (Agarito), 75
Agave, 75
Agave spp., 75
Ageratum, 114
Ageratum spp., 114
Aleppo pine, 68
Allium spp., 124
Almond verbena, 139
Aloysia virgata, 139
Althea, 75
Alyssum, 114
Amaranth, globe, 114
Amaryllis, hardy, 115
American beautyberry, 76
American elm, 49
Anacua, 40
Angel's trumpet, 115
Anisacanthus wrightii, 126
Anise, 76
Anise sage, 136
Annual planting, 14–15
Annuals, perennials, and herbs: fertilizing, 25; mulching, 24; pest control, 25; pruning, 24; watering, 25; weed control, 25
Annuals and perennials reference, 140
Antigonon leptopus, 102
Antirrhinum spp., 137
April maintenance, 30
Aquilegia spp., 119
Aralia, 76

Ardisia, 101
Ardisia japonica, 101
Aromatic sumac, 95
Asclepias tuberosa, 117
Ash, green, 41
Ash, prickly, 41
Ash, Texas, 41
Asian (Asiatic) Jasmine, 105
Aspidistra, 76
Aspidistra elatior, 76
Aster, 115
Aster frikartii, 115
Aucuba, 77
Aucuba japonica, 77
August maintenance, 34
Autumn sage, 136
Azalea, 77
Azalea planting, 13

B

Bacillus thuringiensis (Bt), 20
Backfill, 10
Bald cypress, 47
Bamboo, 78
Bambusa spp., 78
Banana, 78
Banana shrub, 78
Barbados cherry, 79
Bauhinia congesta, 65
Bay, 79
Bay magnolia, 56
Beaked yucca, 98
Beautyberry, 76
Bed preparation, 13
Bee brush, 55
Begonia, 116
Begonia spp., 116
Berberis trifoliata, 75
Bermudagrass, 142
Betula nigra, 42
Bigelow oak, 60
Bigleaf magnolia, 56
Bignonia capreolata, 103
Biodiversity, 8
Birch, river, 42
Bird of paradise, 42
Black cherry, 45
Black-eyed Susan, 116, 122
Black gum, 42

Black haw, 71
Black locust, 55
Black walnut, 72
Bluebonnet, 116
Blue butterfly flower, 116
Blue lily of the Nile, 114
Blue palm, 91
Blue palmetto, 91
Blue plumbago, 132
Blue potato vine, 101
Blue sage, 136
Blue yucca, 99
Boston ivy, 104
Bottlebrush, 79
Bougainvillea, 101
Bougainvillea spp., 101
Boxwood, 80
Brassica oleracea, 127
Brazilian sky flower, 83
Bridal wreath, 95
Brugmansia arborea, 115
Buckeye, Mexican, 43
Buckeye, Texas, 43
Buckthorn, Carolina, 80
Buddleia spp., 80
Bulbine, 117
Bulbine frutescens, 117
Bulb planting, 14
Bumelia lanuginosa, 46
Bur oak, 59
Bush morning glory, 117
Butterfly bush, 80
Butterfly ginger, 125
Butterfly iris, 127
Butterfly weed, 117
Buttonbush, 81
Buxus microphylla, 80

C

Caesalpinia gilliesii, 42
Caesalpinia pulcherrima, 134
Caladium, 117
Caladium spp., 117
Callicarpa americana, 76
Callirhoe involucrata, 139
Callistemon citrinus, 79
Calocedrus decurrens, 45
Calyptocarpus vialis, 104
Camellia, 81

Camellia planting, 13–14
Camellia spp., 81
Camphor tree, 43
Campsis radicans, 110
Canby oak, 59
Candletree, 117
Canna, 118
Canna generalis, 118
Canyon oak, 60
Carissa macrocarpa, 90
Carolina basswood, 44
Carolina buckthorn, 80
Carolina cherry, 45
Carolina jessamine, 106
Carolina red maple, 57
Carya illinoinensis, 67
Carya spp., 52
Cassia alata, 117
Cast iron plant, 76
Castor bean, 81
Catalpa, 44
Catalpa bignonioides, 44
Catharanthus roseus, 132
Cedar, Eastern red, 44
Cedar, incense, 45
Cedar elm, 49
Century plant, 75
Cephalanthus occidentalis, 81
Cercis canadensis, 69
Cestrum auranticum, 98
Chaenomeles japonica, 93
Chalk maple, 56
Chasmanthium latifolium, 143
Chaste tree, 71
Chenille plant, 118
Cherry, black, 45
Cherry, choke, 45
Cherry, wild, 45
Cherry bomb holly, 85
Cherry laurel, 45
Chilopsis linearis, 72
Chinese elm, 50
Chinese fringe flower, 82
Chinese fringe tree, 51
Chinese holly, 87
Chinese photinia, 92
Chinese pistache, 68
Chinese pistachio, 68
Chinese varnish tree, 66

Chinese wisteria, 112
Chinkapin (Chinquapin) oak, 59
Chionanthus virginicus, 51
Chisos oak, 63
Chittamwood, 46
Choke cherry, 45
Chrysanthemum, 118
Chrysanthemum leucanthemum, 122
Chrysanthemum spp., 118
Cigar plant, 118
Cigar tree, 44
Cinnamomum camphora, 43
Citrus, 46
Clematis, fall, 102
Clematis maximowicziana, 102
Clerodendrum ugandense, 116
Clethra, 46
Clethra pringlei, 46
Cleyera, 82
Climbing fig, 105
Coastal live oak, 61
Codiaeum variegatum, 82
Coleus, 119
Coleus hybrids, 119
Columbine, 119
Common persimmon, 67
Compost, 5
Coneflower, 122
Coneflower, purple, 119
Coneflower, yellow, 119
Confederate jasmine, 106
Cool-season grass planting, 17
Copper Canyon daisy, 121
Copperleaf, 119
Copper plant, 119
Coral bark maple, 57
Coral bean, 120
Coral fountain, 124
Coral honeysuckle, 103
Coral plant, 124
Coral vine, 102
Cordia boissieri, 64
Coreopsis, 120
Coreopsis spp., 120
Cornmeal, 6
Corn poppy, 133
Cornus drummondii, 49
Cornus florida, 48
Cortaderia selloana, 144
Cosmos, 120
Cosmos spp., 120
Crape myrtle, 46
Crape myrtle, dwarf, 82
Crataegus marshallii, 52

Creeping fig, 105
Creeping thyme, 110
Crimson queen Japanese maple, 57
Crossvine, 103
Croton, 82
Crow flower, 133
Cuphea hyssopifolia, 129
Cuphea ignea, 118
Cup oak, 59
Cycas revoluta, 94
Cyclamen, 120
Cyclamen spp., 120
Cynodon dactylon, 142
Cyperus, 83
Cyperus alternifolius, 83
Cypress, bald, 47
Cypress, Montezuma, 47
Cypress, pond, 48
Cyrtomium falcatum, 84

D
Daffodil, 121
Daisy, Copper Canyon, 121
Daisy, four-nerve, 121
Daisy, gerbera, 121
Daisy, oxeye, 122
Darlington oak, 60
Date palm, 66
Datura, 115
Dawn redwood, 69
Daylily, 122
Dead man's fingers, 133
December maintenance, 38
Desert willow, 72
Diamondleaf oak, 60
Dianthus, 123
Dianthus spp., 123
Dietes spp., 127
Diospyros texana, 67
Diospyros virginiana, 67
Diplolaena dampieri, 84
Dogwood, flowering, 48
Dogwood, rough-leaf, 49
Dragon lily, 131
Drainage, 10
Drake elm, 50
Drummond red maple, 57
Drunken sailor, 109
Dryopteris spp., 84
Duck oak, 63
Durand oak, 60
Duranta, 83
Duranta spp., 83
Dwarf Burford holly, 86

Dwarf Chinese holly, 86
Dwarf monkey grass, 108
Dwarf palm, 91
Dwarf palmetto, 91
Dwarf yaupon holly, 86

E
Eastern red cedar, 44
Echinacea angustifolia, 119
Edible peach, 66
Egg flower, 133
Ehretia anacua, 40
Elaeagnus, 83
Elm, American, 49
Elm, cedar, 49
Elm, Chinese, 50
Elm, evergreen, 50
Elm, lacebark, 50
Elm, Siberian, 50
Elm, winged, 50
English holly, 87
English ivy, 104
Equisetum hyemale, 88
Eriobotrya japonica, 89
Erythrina herbacea, 120
Esperanza, 123
Euonymus americana, 138
Euonymus fortunei, 111
Euonymus radicans, 111
Eupatorium greggii, 130
Euphorbia, 123
Euphorbia 'Diamond frost', 123
Evening primrose, 134
Evergreen elm, 50
Evergreen sumac, 95
Evergreen wisteria, 112
Eve's necklace, 50
Expanded shale, 7
Eysenhardtia texana, 55

F
Fall-blooming aster, 115
Fall clematis, 102
Fall spider lily, 138
False heather, 129
False Japanese yew, 93
Fan palm, 66
Fatsia japonica, 76
Feather duster, 84
February maintenance, 28
Feijoa, 92
Feijoa sellowiana, 92
Fern, holly, 84
Fern, wood, 84
Fertilizer, 7, 19

Fescue, 142
Festuca arundinacea, 142
Ficus pumila, 105
Fig ivy, 105
Firebush, 124
Firecracker fern, 124
Firmiana simplex, 66
Fish bait tree, 44
Flame acanthus, 126
Flameleaf sumac, 96
Florida anise, 76
Florida maple, 58
Flowering cabbage, 127
Flowering dogwood, 48
Flowering kale, 127
Flowering quince, 93
Flower planting, 14
Flowers, 3
Fly tree, 71
Forest pansy redbud, 69
Forked-leaf white oak, 63
Foster holly, 53, 87
Fountain grass, 143
Fountain plant, 124
Four-nerve daisy, 121
Fragrant sumac, 95
Frangipani, 133
Fraxinus pennsylvanica, 41
Fraxinus texensis, 41
Fringe flower, Chinese, 82
Fringe tree, 51

G
Galphimia glauca, 97
Gardenia, 85
Gardenia jasminoides, 85
Gardenia planting, 13
Garlic, 124
Gaura, 124
Gaura lindheimeri, 124
Gayfeather, 124
Gazania, 125
Gazania hybrids, 125
Gelsemium sempervirens, 106
Geranium, 125
Gerbera daisy, 121
Gerbera jamesonii, 121
Germander, 85
Gill ivy, 105
Ginger, butterfly, 125
Ginkgo, 51
Ginkgo biloba, 51
Gladiola, hardy, 125
Gladiolus byzantinus, 125
Glauconite, 6

Glechoma hederacea, 105
Globe, amaranth, 114
Gloriosa daisy, 122
Goldenrain tree, 52
Gold star esperanza, 123
Gomphrena globosa, 114
Grape, 103
Grass, 4; aeration, 27; fertilizing, 26; hydromulching, 16–17; maintenance, 26; maintenance mistakes, 27; pest control, 27; planting, 16; seeding, 16–17; solid sod planting, 17; spot-sodding, 17; watering, 26
Green ash, 41
Greensand, 6
Gregg salvia, 136
Gregg's mistflower, 130
Ground cover reference, 112
Ground covers, 3, 12
Ground covers and vines: fertilizing, 24; mulching, 24; pest control, 24; pruning, 23; watering, 24
Ground ivy, 105
Guava, 92
Guavasteen, 92

H
Hamamelis virginiana, 73
Hamelia patens, 124
Hardy amaryllis, 115
Hardy gladiola, 125
Hawthorn, parsley, 52
Heavenly bamboo, 90
Hedera colchica, 105
Hedera helix, 104
Hedychium coronarium, 125
Hemerocallis spp., 122
Herbs, 3
Hesperaloe parviflora, 99
Hibiscus, 125
Hibiscus syriacus, 75
Hickory, 52
Hippeastrum × *johnsonii,* 115
Hog plum, 69
Holly, cherry bomb, 85
Holly, dwarf Burford, 86
Holly, dwarf Chinese, 86
Holly, dwarf yaupon, 86
Holly, 'East Palatka', 53
Holly, Foster, 53, 87
Holly, Nellie R. Stevens, 87
Holly, oak leaf, 87

Holly, Savannah, 54
Holly, Wirt L. Winn, 87
Holly, yaupon, 54
Holly, yaupon deciduous, 53
Holly fern, 84
Honeysuckle, coral, 103
Horseherb, 104
Horsetail reed, 88
Hummingbird bush, 126
Hurricane lily, 131
Hyacinth, 126
Hyacinthus spp., 126
Hydrangea, 88
Hydrangea, florist, 88
Hydrangea, oak leaf, 88
Hydrangea macrophylla, 88
Hydrangea quercifolia, 88
Hymenocallis liriosme, 138
Hymenoxys, 121

I
Iceland poppy, 133
Ilex cornuta 'Burfordii Nana', 86
Ilex cornuta 'Rotunda', 86
Ilex decidua, 53
Ilex opaca x *attenuata,* 54
Ilex vomitoria 'Nana', 54, 86
Ilex × *attenuata* 'East Palatka', 53
Ilex × *attenuata* 'Foster', 87
Ilex × 'Cherry Bomb', 85
Ilex × Nellie R. Stevens, 87
Impatiens, 126
Impatiens spp., 126
Incense cedar, 45
Indian bean, 44
Indian cherry, 80
Indian spice, 71
Inland seaoats, 143
Iochroma, 127
Ipomoea fistulosa, 117
Ipomoea spp., 108
Iris, 127
Iris spp., 127
Iron crossvine, 103
Italian jasmine, 88
Itea virginica, 98
Ivy, Boston, 104
Ivy, English, 104
Ivy, fig, 105
Ivy, gill, 105
Ivy, ground, 105
Ivy, Persian, 105

J
Jacob's ladder, 125

January maintenance, 28
Japanese ardisia, 101
Japanese holly fern, 84
Japanese maple, 57
Japanese maple, crimson queen, 57
Japanese persimmon
Japanese star jasmine, 105
Japanese virburnum, 97
Japanese yew, 93
Jasmine, Asian, 105
Jasmine, Confederate, 106
Jasmine, Italian, 88
Jasminum humile, 88
Jerusalem sage, 136
Jessamine, Carolina, 106
Johnny-jump-ups, 131
Jonquil, 121
Juglans nigra, 72
Jujube, 54
July maintenance, 33
June maintenance, 32
Juniperus virginiana, 44
Justicia brandegeana, 137

K
Kale, 127
Katie ruellia, 129
Kidneywood, Texas, 55
Koelreuteria paniculata, 52

L
Lacebark elm, 50
Lacevine, silver, 106
Lacey oak, 60
Lady in the bark, 109
Lagerstroemia indica, 46, 82
Lantana, 128
Lantana spp., 128
Laurel leaf oak, 60
Laurel oak, 60, 63
Laurus nobilis, 79
Leather leaf mahonia, 89
Liatris spp., 124
Ligularia, 128
Lilac chaste tree, 71
Lily of the Nile, 114
Lilyturf, 107
Liquidambar styraciflua, 70
Liriodendron tulipifera, 71
Liriope, 107
'Little gem' magnolia, 56
Live oak, 61
Loblolly pine, 68
Lobularia maritime, 114

Locust, black, 55
Lonicera sempervirens, 103
Loquat, 89
Loquat, coppertone, 89
Loropetalum, 82
Loropetalum chinense, 82
Lupinus texensis, 116
Lycoris radiata, 131
Lycoris spp., 138

M
Magnolia, bay, 56
Magnolia, bigleaf, 56
Magnolia, 'little gem', 56
Magnolia, saucer, 55
Magnolia, southern, 55
Magnolia, star, 55
Magnolia grandiflora, 55
Magnolia soulangiana, 56
Magnolia stellata, 56
Magnolia virginiana, 56
Mahonia bealei, 89
Mahonia gracilis, 89
Mahonia, leather leaf, 89
Maidenhair tree, 51
Maintenance by the calendar, 28
Malpighia glabra, 79
Malus spp., 46
Malvaviscus arboreus, 97
Mandevilla, 107
Mandevilla × 'Alice du Pont', 107
Manzanita, 79
Maple, chalk, 56
Maple, coral bark, 57
Maple, Drummond red, 57
Maple, Florida, 58
Maple, Japanese, 57
Maple, Japanese 'Crimson Queen', 57
Maple, Japanese 'Orangeola', 57
Maple, scarlet, 57
Maple, soft, 57
Maple, southern sugar, 58
Maple, swamp, 57
Maple, trident, 58
Maple, water, 57
March maintenance, 29
Marigold, 128
May maintenance, 31
Maypops, 108
McFarland, Dr. Joe, 6
Mealy blue sage, 136
Melochia, 128
Melochia tomentosa, 128
Mentha spp., 107

Metasequoia glyptostroboides, 69
Mexican buckeye, 43
Mexican bush salvia, 136
Mexican clethra, 46
Mexican firebush, 124
Mexican heather, 129
Mexican mint marigold, 129
Mexican oak, 61
Mexican oregano, 129
Mexican petunia, 129
Mexican plum, 69
Mexican redbud, 69
Mexican sycamore, 70
Meyer lemon, 46
Michelia skinneriana, 78
Miniature lily, 131
Mineral content (soil), 8
Mint, 107
Miscanthus spp., 143
Mistflower, 130
Mock orange, 90
Molasses, 7, 8
Monarda, 130
Monarda spp., 130
Mondo grass, 108
Monkey grass, 107
Monterrey oak, 61
Montezuma cypress, 47
Morea bicolor, 127
Morning glory, 108
Moss phlox, 138
Mossy oak, 59
Mountain laurel, Texas, 70
Mountain sage, 136
Mowing, 26
Mowing heights, 26
Muhlenbergia capillaris, 143
Muhly, Gulf Coast, 143
Mulches/mulching, 7, 19;
    annuals and perennials, 14
Mum, 118
Musa spp., 78
Myrica cerifera, 72
Myrtle, wax, 72

N
Nandina, 90
Nandina domestica, 90
Narcissus spp., 121
Nasturtium, 130
Natal plum, 90
Needle palm, 65, 66
Needlepoint holly, 86
Nellie R. Stevens holly, 87
Northern pin oak, 62

November maintenance, 37
N-P-K, 7
Nutrients, 5
Nuttall oak, 62
Nyssa sylvatica, 42

O
Oak, Bigalow, 60
Oak, bur, 59
Oak, Canby, 59
Oak, canyon, 60
Oak, Chinkapin, 59
Oak, Chisos, 63
Oak, cup, 59
Oak, Durand, 60
Oak, lacey, 60
Oak, laurel, 60
Oak, live, 61
Oak, Mexican, 61
Oak, mossy, 59
Oak, Nuttall, 62
Oak, post, 62
Oak, smokey, 60
Oak, Southern red, 62
Oak, Texas red, 62
Oak, water, 63
Oak, white, 63
Oak, willow, 64
Oak leaf holly, 87
Oak wilt control, 21
Obtusa oak, 60
October maintenance, 36
Oenothera spp., 134
Oklahoma redbud, 69
Oleander, 91
Olive, wild, 64
Ophiopogon, 108
Ophiopogon japonicus, 108
Opium poppy, 133
Orange, trifoliate, 64
Orangeola maple, 57
Orchid tree, 65
Organic matter, 5–6, 8
Oriental poppy, 133
Osmanthus americanus, 96
Oxblood lily, 130
Oxeye daisy, 122

P
Palm, sabal minor, 91
Palm, Texas, 65
Pampas grass, 144
Pansy, 131
Papaver spp., 133
Parasol tree, 66

Parsleyleaf hawthorn, 52
Parthenocissus quinquefolia, 111
Parthenocissus tricuspidata, 104
Paspalum, 144
Paspalum vaginatum, 144
Passion vine, 108
Pavonia, 131
Pavonia peruviensis, 131
Peach, 66
Peach, flowering, 66
Pecan, 67
Pelargonium hortorum, 125
Pennisetum spp., 143
Penstemon, 131
Penstemon spp., 131
Pentas, 131
Pentas lanceolata, 131
Pepper tree, 71
Perennial planting, 14–15
Periwinkle, 132
Perovskia atriplicifolia, 136
Persian ivy, 105
Persimmon, common, 67
Persimmon, Texas, 67
Peruvian pavonia, 131
Pest control, 20; for shrubs, 23
Petunia, 132
Petunia × hybrida, 132
Philadelphus, 90
Philadelphus spp., 90
Philodendron, split-leaf, 91
Phlomis fruticosa, 136
Phlox, 132
Phlox spp., 132
Phlox subulata, 138
Photinia, Chinese, 92
Photinia serrulata, 92
Pickerel rush, 132
Pigmy date palm, 66
Pignut hickory, 53
Pindo palm, 66
Pine, 68
Pineapple guava, 92
Pink skullcap, 137
Pin oak, 62, 64
Pinus taeda, 68
Pistache, Chinese, 68
Pistache, Texas, 68
Pistacia chinensis, 68
Pistacia texana, 68
Pittosporum, 92
Pittosporum tobira, 92
Planting depths, 11
Planting times, 9
Plum, hog, 69

Plum, Mexican, 69
Plumbago, 132
Plumbago auriculata, 132
Plum delight, 82
Plumeria, 133
Plumeria spp., 133
Podocarpus, 93
Podocarpus macrophyllus, 93
Poisonous plants, 4
Poliomintha longiflora, 129
Polygonum aubertii, 106
Pomegranate, 93
Poncirus trifoliata, 64
Pond cypress, 48
Pontederia cordata, 132
Poor man's orchid, 122
Poplar, tulip, 71
Poppy, 133
Portulaca, 133
Portulaca grandiflora, 133
Possum oak, 63
Post oak, 62
Prairie flameleaf sumac, 96
Prickly ash, 41
Pride of Barbados, 134
Primrose, 134
Prostrate lawnflower, 104
Pruning, 12
Prunus caroliniana, 45
Prunus mexicana, 69
Prunus serotina, 45
Punica granatum, 93
Purple anise, 76
Purple coneflower, 119
Purple heart, 109
Purple queen, 109
Purple wandering Jew, 109
Purple winter creeper, 111
Purslane, 134
Pyramid bush, 128

Q
Queen palm, 66
Quercus alba, 63
Quercus canbyi, 59
Quercus falcata, 62
Quercus glaucoides, 60
Quercus gravesii, 63
Quercus laceyi, 60
Quercus laurifolia, 60
Quercus macrocarpa, 59
Quercus muhlenbergii, 59
Quercus nigra, 63
Quercus nuttallii, 62
Quercus phellos, 64

Quercus polymorpha, 61
Quercus shumardii, 62
Quercus sinuata, 60
Quercus stellata, 62
Quercus texana, 62
Quercus virginiana, 61
Quince, flowering, 93
Quisqualis indica, 109

R
Rain lily, 134
Rangoon creeper, 109
Rangoon vine, 109
Redbud, 69
Red maple, 57
Red oak, 62
Red River oak, 62
Red spider lily, 138
Redwood, dawn, 69
Red yucca, 99
Reference for annuals and perennials, 140
Reference for ground covers and vines, 112
Reference for shrubs, 100
Reference for trees, 73
Rhamnus caroliniana, 80
Rhododendron, 94
Rhododendron planting, 13
Rhododendron spp., 77, 94
Rhodophiala bifida, 130
Rhus aromatica, 95
Rhus copallina, 96
Rhus glabra, 96
Rhus virens, 95
Rice paper plant, 94
Rich oak, 60
Ricinus communis, 81
River birch, 42
Robinia pseudoacacia, 55
Rosa spp., 134
Rosemary, 135
Rose of Sharon, 75
Rosmarinus officinalis, 135
Rough-leaf dogwood, 49
Rudbeckia hirta, 122
Ruellia spp., 129
Russelia spp., 124

S
Sabal mexicana, 65
Sabal minor palm, 91
Sabal palm, 65
Sage, 136
Sage tree, 71

Sago palm, 66, 94
Salvia, 136
Salvia farinacea, 136
Salvia greggii, 136
Satsuma mandarin, 46
Satsuma orange, 46
Saucer magnolia, 55
Savannah holly, 54
Scalping, 26
Scarlet bush, 124
Scarlet maple, 57
Scarlet rangoon, 109
Scarlet sage, 136
Schoolhouse lily, 130
Scutellaria suffrutescens, 137
Sedum, 109
Sedum spp., 109
September maintenance, 35
Setcreasea pallida, 109
Shale, 7
Shining sumac, 96
Short leaf pine, 68
Shrimp plant, 137
Shrub reference, 100
Shrubs, 3, 12; fertilizing, 23; mulching, 22; pruning, 22; watering, 23
Shumard red oak, 62
Siberian elm, 50
Sick tree treatment, 21
Silverberry, 83
Silver lacevine, 106
Skinner's banana shrub, 78
Skullcap, 137
Skunkbush, 95
Slash pine, 68
Smokey oak, 60
Smooth sumac, 96
Snapdragon, 137
Society garlic, 124
Soft maple, 57
Soil amendments, 5–6
Soils, 5
Solanum spp., 101
Sophora affinis, 50
Sophora secundiflora, 70
Southern magnolia, 55
Southern red oak, 62
Southern sugar maple, 58
Spider lily, 138
Spiraea, 95
Spirea spp., 95
Split-leaf philodendron, 91
Spotted oak, 63
Staking, 12

Star anise, 76
Star magnolia, 55
St. Augustinegrass, 145
Stenotaphrum secundatum, 145
Stink-bush, 76
St. Joseph's lily, 115
Straggler daisy, 104
Strawberry bush, 138
Striped oak, 62
Sumac, evergreen, 95
Sumac, flameleaf, 96
Sumac, smooth, 96
Summer lilac
Swamp bay, 56
Swamp laurel oak, 60
Swamp magnolia, 56
Swamp mallow, 125
Swamp maple, 57
Swamp willow oak, 64
Sweet alyssum, 114
Sweet bay, 79
Sweet bay magnolia, 56
Sweetgum, 70
Sweet marigold, 129
Sweet olive, 96
Sycamore, Mexican, 70

T
Tagetes lemmonii, 121
Tagetes lucida, 129
Tagetes spp., 128
Taxodium ascendens, 48
Taxodium distichum, 47
Taxodium mucronatum, 47
Tea bush, 128
Tecoma stans, 123
Ternstroemia gymnanthera, 82
Tetraneuris scaposa, 121
Tetrapanax papyriferus, 94
Teucrium spp., 85
Texas ash, 41
Texas buckeye, 43
Texas kidneywood, 55
Texas mountain laurel, 70
Texas palm, 65
Texas persimmon, 67
Texas pistache, 68
Texas red oak, 62
Texas sophora, 50
Thrift, 138
Thryallis, 97
Thunbergia alata, 116
Thyme, creeping, 110
Thymus spp., 110
Tilia caroliniana, 44

Toothache tree, 41
Trachelospermum asiaticum, 105
Trachelospermum jasminoides, 106
Trachelospermum mandaianum, 106
Transplanting, 14
Transvaal daisy, 121
Tree maintenance, 18
Tree mulch, 12
Tree planting, 9, 10
Tree pruning, 18
Tree reference list, 73
Trees, 2, 40
Trident maple, 57, 58
Trifoliate orange, 64
Tropaeolum majus, 130
Trumpet vine, 110
Tulbaghia violacea, 124
Tulip of the South, 115
Tulip poplar, 71
Tulip tree, 71
Turk's cap, 97

U
Ulmus alata, 50
Ulmus americana, 49
Ulmus crassifolia, 49
Ulmus parvifolia sempervirens, 50
Ulmus pumila, 50
Umbrella plant, 83
Ungnadia speciosa, 43

V
Varnish tree, 66
Verbena, 139
Verbena, almond, 139
Verbena spp., 139
Viburnum, Japanese, 97
Viburnum, rusty blackhaw, 71
Viburnum, Walter, 98
Viburnum obovatum, 98
Viburnum odoratissimum, 97
Viburnum rufidulum, 71
Vinca, 111
Vinca major, 111
Vinca minor, 111
Vine reference, 112–113
Vines, 3, 12
Viola hybrids, 131
Violas, 131
Virginia creeper, 111
Virginia sweetspire, 98
Vitex, 71
Vitex agnus-castus, 71
Vitis spp., 103

W

Walnut, black, 72
Walter's viburnum, 98
Water birch, 42
Watering, 20
Water larch, 47
Water maple, 57
Water oak, 63
Water saving tips, 27
Wax myrtle, 72
Weed control, 16, 21, 23
Weeping yaupon holly, 54
White bark maple, 56
White oak, 63
White spider lily, 131, 138

Whitewood, 71
Wild cherry, 45
Wild flower planting, 16
Wild oats, 143
Wild olive, 64
Willow leaf holly, 86
Willow oak, 64
Willow, desert, 72
Windmill palm, 65, 66
Winecup, 139
Winged elm, 50
Winter creeper, 111
Wirt L. Winn holly, 87
Wisteria, Chinese, 112
Witch hazel, 73

Wood fern, 84

Y

Yarrow, 139
Yaupon holly, 54
Yellow bells (Agarita), 123
Yellow bells (Esperanza), 75
Yellow cestrum, 98
Yellow jasmine, 106
Yellow pine, 68
Yellow poplar, 71
Yellow shrub jasmine, 98
Yucca, beaked, 98
Yucca, red, 99
Yucca, soft, 99

Yucca gloriosa, 99
Yucca rigida, 99
Yucca rostrata, 98
Yucca rupicola, 99

Z

Zanthoxylum clava-herculis, 41
Zephyranthes spp., 134
Zinnia, 140
Zinnia spp., 140
Ziziphus spp., 54
Zoysiagrass, 145
Zoysia japonica, 145